THE WHITE PLUME

A Pictorial Representation of the Steam Locomotive

BY CHARLES BOWMAN

A **Railfare** Book

Book design by David R. Henderson
Copyright 1976 by Railfare Enterprises Limited
All rights reserved
Published by Henry Regnery Company
180 North Michigan Avenue, Chicago, Illinois 60601
Manufactured in Canada
Library of Congress Catalog Card Number: 76-25349
International Standard Book Number: 0-8092-7911-8

Photograph by George Riley

Charles William Robertson Bowman

PUBLISHER'S PREFACE

To THE INTENSE SORROW of his family and friends, Charles William Robertson Bowman passed away suddenly in December 1974 while on vacation with his beloved wife, Patricia. He had completed work on the manuscript and illustrations of this book just a short time previously, and had but recently returned from a trip to Austria and its neighbouring countries, gathering material for a planned further book on his favourite subject, the steam locomotive.

The publishers' desire to complete the book as a posthumous tribute to a person whose talents — not merely as a photographer but as a photographic artist — were widely acknowledged, was unreservedly supported by Mrs. Bowman. Moreover, at her suggestion, the manuscript has been supplemented by a small selection of photographs taken during the Bowmans' 1974 trip to Austria. Such an addition is especially appropriate since it enables the artistic continuity of the book to be preserved by utilizing photographs edited and printed personally by Charles Bowman shortly before his death.

The photographs were selected by Mrs. Bowman in consultation with Omer Lavallée, who has prepared the text of Chapter Six from Mr. Bowman's notes supplemented by his personal familiarity with Austria and its railways.

Charles Bowman's knowledge and love of his subject are apparent in this tribute to the steam locomotive. That he was an internationalist with cosmopolitan tastes contributed immeasurably to his enjoyment of his hobby. *The White Plume* bears testimony to the concept that the steam locomotive, though born in England, belongs to the world.

One of the impressive aspects of the author's photography is the fact that all of it is in his preferred format, 35 mm. His meticulously-filed and annotated collections of negatives and prints, destined hopefully to provide illustrations for future texts, testify to the abilities of one who was at once an exacting professional engineer, a versatile and adept photographer and an indefatigable traveller.

Most of all, he was a kind, amiable and good-natured human being, and that is how his friends will remember Charles Bowman.

4:
The diminutive *Prince* of the 60-cm. gauge Festiniog
Railway in North Wales trails a long "white plume" as
it moves a passenger carriage across the embankment
known as *The Cob* between Portmadoc and Boston
Lodge Works on 15 May 1968.

CONTENTS

DEDICATION

This book is dedicated to the vast number of people in many lands who have made railways a fascinating factor in our lives — those who designed, financed, and built them, those who operate and maintain them, those who travel on them and those who make use of them for movement of goods and livestock — and without whom there would be no railways.

ACKNOWLEDGEMENTS

My thanks are due to the several railway authorities who graciously provided lineside and depot permits; to signalmen who were always willing to have me up in the box for a chat and to provide useful information on train working and equipment; to locomotive foremen and shedmasters who gave me the run of the shed for photography and on occasion had a few engines moved around to improve the composition; to engine crews who were willing to have me in the cab; to many friends who passed along word of special workings; and, last but by no means least, to the women in my life — my mother who was prepared to sit for hours in Princes Street Gardens in Edinburgh while I "watched trains" as a boy and my wife Patricia who has been even more tolerant to the extent of missing meals and spending days at the lineside during holidays. Often she handles the sound while I am photographing or does colour while I handle black-and-white. A close bachelor friend, who shall remain nameless, once remarked on seeing some of Patricia's slides "If I could find a girl who could take railway pictures like that, I'd get married!"

I am deeply grateful to all of these people for their help in making possible this pictorial presentation of the steam locomotive and especially to Omer Lavallée, my good friend who encouraged me to do it.

Dollard des Ormeaux
Quebec, Canada   1974   C.W.R. Bowman

INTRODUCTION

WHILE THE GREY HAZE of a properly fired engine on a warm day is undoubtedly very satisfying to the locomotive inspector and a pall of black smoke provides dramatic effect for the photographer, the white plume symbolizes the whole essence of the steam locomotive.

Whether it is being blasted skywards in great billows by a hard working freight engine, hissing deafeningly from safety valves as if to defy any boiler to contain it, or streaking back behind a fast-moving Pacific, the fascination is the same — an inexplicable fascination that seems to be something with which one is born.

The Canadian section of the book depicts mainly preserved locomotives in the east. The far-sightedness of Canadian National and the support of railway societies in keeping one steam locomotive in working order for excursion service throughout the sixties and up to the present time has enabled a sampling of the Canadian railway scene to be included. With considerable cooperation from CP Rail, the recently-formed Ontario Rail Association has restored two Canadian Pacific locomotives to operating condition and these are now available for special trips from their home depot at John Street, Toronto. Perhaps this limited number of locomotive types offers a greater challenge in obtaining pictures which are not repetitious.

When factors such as weather, coal quality, driving and firing methods are considered, coupled with the great variety of engine types, the photographic possibilities which can result from steam locomotives are seemingly endless.

It is this variety that has promoted this book. The photographs, extending into the preservation era, do not cover comprehensively any particular country, railway or region of a railway; neither do they deal with particular types of locomotive or any specific class. The locations are varied; some were discovered fortuitously; others were diligently searched out for one reason or another; a few were found because I had previously seen pictures in the general area; others resulted from just being at that spot when a train came along. There is but one unifying theme — steam, and its incredible fascination.

6:
British Rail Hall class 4-6-0 5984 *Linden Hall* restarts a northbound freight after a signal check at the junctions south of Cheltenham, England in June 1963.

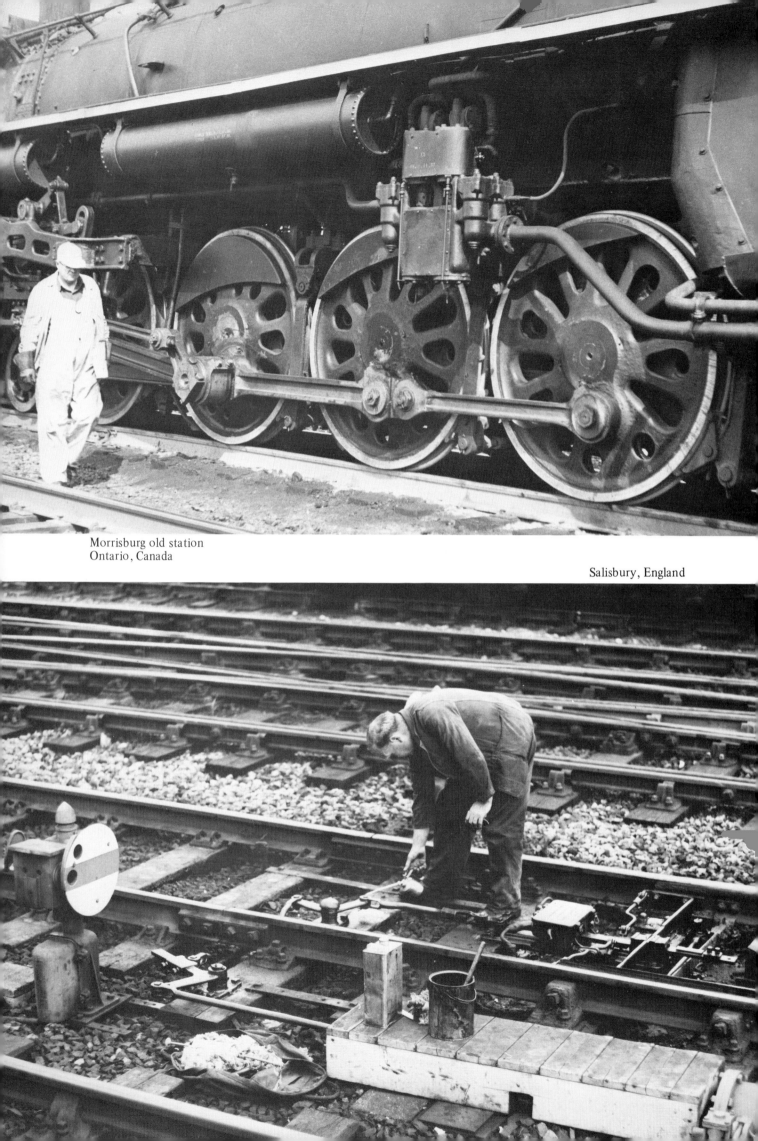

Morrisburg old station
Ontario, Canada

Salisbury, England

1 WITHOUT WHOM THERE WOULD BE NO RAILWAYS

Banbury mpd
England

Rheine Bw
West Germany

York, England

Eskdale Green, England

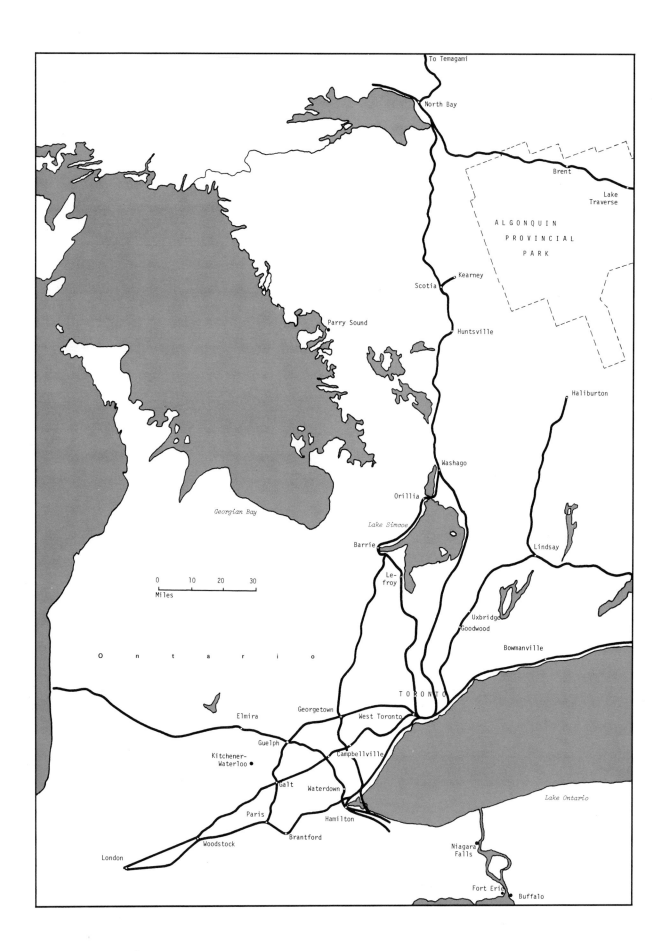

To Temagami

North Bay

Brent

Lake
Traverse

A L G O N Q U I N

P R O V I N C I A L

P A R K

Kearney

Scotia

Huntsville

Haliburton

Parry Sound

Washago

Orillia

Georgian Bay

Lake Simcoe

Lindsay

Barrie

Le-
froy

Uxbridge

Goodwood

Bowmanville

O   n   t   a   r   i   o

T O R O N T O

Elmira

Georgetown

West Toronto

Guelph

Campbellville

Kitchener-
Waterloo

Galt

Waterdown

Lake Ontario

Paris

Hamilton

Brantford

Niagara
Falls

Woodstock

London

Fort Erie

Buffalo

0   10   20   30
Miles

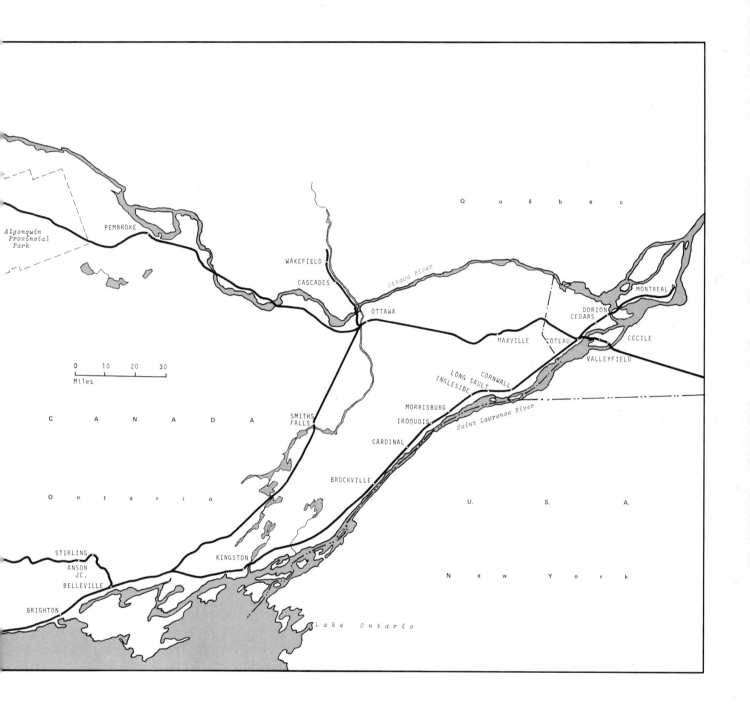

Algonquin
Provincial
Park

PEMBROKE

Q u é b e c

WAKEFIELD

CASCADES

Ottawa River

OTTAWA

MONTREAL

DORION
CEDARS

MAXVILLE   COTEAU

CECILE

VALLEYFIELD

0   10   20   30
Miles

C A N A D A

CORNWALL
LONG SAULT
INGLESIDE

SMITHS
FALLS

MORRISBURG

IROQUOIS

Saint Lawrence River

CARDINAL

O n t a r i o

BROCKVILLE

U.   S.   A.

STIRLING

ANSON
JC.

BELLEVILLE

KINGSTON

N e w   Y o r k

BRIGHTON

L a k e   O n t a r i o

CANADA
AND U.S.A.

14:
The Moccasin was the name applied locally to the CN early morning train from Brockville and Montreal (No. 26) and its evening return (No. 25). The usual consist was two baggage cars, a combine and a coach and it carried more express and mail than passengers although in the late Fifties it was still well patronized. It was very handy for getting to Montreal for a day's shopping especially for passengers from Cornwall, where it called around 0730, and points eastwards. Construction of the St. Lawrence Seaway and Power Project necessitated re-routing of the Montreal-Toronto main line between Cornwall and Cardinal, Ontario as parts of the railway passed through areas which would be flooded. Class J-7-b Pacific 5283 with No. 26 has just topped the rise between Moulinette and Mille Roches on a warm summer morning in July 1957 shortly before closure of the old line.

15:
The Moccasin like so many other local trains was an integral part of the life of the people along the line. It stopped at nearly every station and slowed to a crawl at obscure road crossings to drop off a bag of mail to a waiting car which presumably took it to some small country post office. Although it ran smartly between stops its overall pace was leisurely and its stops were often lengthy. The evening train brought cartons of bread from Montreal to Cornwall, although one wonders why as an excellent local product was baked by Riley's on Pitt Street. J-7-b Pacifics were the usual power for the Moccasin in the late Fifties. On an August morning in 1957 not long after the 40-mile diversion was opened to traffic, 5280, one of the regulars, whistles for the Mille Roches Road crossing, between Long Sault (a new name on the CN map) and Cornwall with Train No.26.

16:
A U-1-f as it ought to look. The doyen of the class, CN 6060, in July 1973 during a test steaming at Point St. Charles shops in Montreal subsequent to complete restoration by Canadian National. A long blast on the whistle seems to be a bit much for David Jordan's young ears!

This locomotive, after withdrawal from regular service, was placed on static display at Jasper, Alberta in 1962 and remained there until 1972 when it was brought east to be given a heavy overhaul and made available for excursion service. It was replaced at Jasper by CN 6015, a 4-8-2 of Class U-1-a, a 1923 design of more conventional appearance.

17:
The Cornwall to Cardinal diversion required the construction of new stations and sidings at Cornwall, Long Sault, Ingleside, Morrisburg and Iroquois. In August 1957, CN 6068, a 4-8-2 of Class U-1-f, heads the westbound Lakeshore Express (No.7) from Montreal to Toronto through Morrisburg with the new track in its first month of use. The U-1-f class was the last new steam locomotive design for CN. All twenty of these handsome Mountains were built by Montreal Locomotive Works in the latter part of 1944 with two 24" x 30" cylinders, 73" drivers and 260 psi boiler pressure. They had flared stacks, but for some reason 6068 acquired a straight version which completely marred the appearance of the engine. It still retains its conical nose which some of the class lost in later years.

18:
CN 6167 became well known in Ontario in the early sixties. This Class U-2-e 4-8-4, built by Montreal Locomotive Works in 1940, had been retained by CN for excursion service and between July 1960 and September 1964 hauled 50 special trains some 12,000 miles. The Royal York Hotel towers over Toronto Union Station as the engineman and conductor look over train orders prior to departure for Picton, Ontario, in August 1962.

19:
A CN excursion from Montreal to Cantic, Quebec, on 14 October 1962 was double headed by J-4-d 4-6-2 5107 and U-2-c 4-8-4 6153. It was the last run for both locomotives prior to withdrawal. The route was via Coteau Junction in both directions and the pair are seen here during the runpast at Mile 38 of the Valleyfield Subdivision on the return journey.

(See map of Quebec area on page 31.)

21:
The near-horizontal rays of the sun glare off CN 5107's tender as the Pacific and the Northern make the last runpast of the day on 14 October 1962. The location is Cecile, Quebec.

20:
Seen from the tender of CN 6153 the two locomotives simmer gently in the dusk after taking water at Valleyfield, Quebec. As is usual on fantrips now that railway water facilities are no longer available, the local fire brigade got in a little pumping practice by filling the tanks from the St. Lawrence River, alongside which the line very conveniently runs at this location. Only the 43 miles to Montreal remain to complete a perfect autumn day — and the operating careers of these two locomotives.

Captions to 22, 23-a and 23-b appear on page 24.

22:

CN 6167 on a winter run from Toronto to Guelph, Galt and Hamilton, Ontario, photographed south of Guelph at Mile 23.3 of the Fergus Subdivision. Steam from the whistle, which is mounted on the left side of the smokebox, conveniently isolates the top of the engine from the background. So, while exuberant use of the whistle during a runpast is not always the desire of the tape recordists, it can have its benefits for the photographers.

23-b:

Probably the most ambitious excursion ever organized by the Upper Canada Railway Society. It ran from Toronto to Ottawa overnight on 13 September 1963 – yes it was a Friday! – and continued to North Bay, Ontario on the Saturday where it spent most of the night. Leaving in the small hours of Sunday 15 September 1963 it headed north to Temagami, returning to North Bay in the forenoon, and finally to Toronto late in the evening. The route covered 840 miles. Sleeping and dining cars were included in the 13-car (!) consist, with four coaches being added between Ottawa and Brent (165 miles) for day trip passengers from the Capital. Except for North Bay to Temagami and return CN 6167 hauled the train throughout. There were seven stops for coal and water and three more for water only. There were 13 runpasts! Despite the recurrence of the supposedly unlucky number, the week-end was an astounding success.

Amid the woodland beauty of Algonquin Park 6167 heads its 17-car train on runpast No. 6 beside the Petawawa River at Mile 145.2 of the Beachburg Subdivision between Lake Traverse and Radiant.

23-a:

Later in September 1963, the Upper Canada Railway Society ran a special to Haliburton, Ontario, from Toronto. This became an annual trip to co-incide with the glorious fall colour in the Haliburton Highlands and was advertised as such. CN 6167 worked the train only as far as Lindsay, as it was not permitted on the Haliburton branch, but the autumn leaves in this scenic part of Ontario must hold some attraction as the passengers always seemed to be having a great time on the branch.

The sun had already set when the last runpast of the day took place at Mile 32, Uxbridge Subdivision. Perhaps wishing to emphasize her presence across the countryside in the failing light (as if the sound wasn't enough), 6167 throws a lot of unburnt coal aloft between Uxbridge and Goodwood.

24:
CN 6218 and CN 6167 turn their train on the wye at Scotia, Ontario, on 26 September 1964.

The destination on that date was Huntsville, in the picturesque Lake of Bays area. A two-hour stop had been scheduled to allow the passengers, 930 of them, to have a look around the town, but during this time the train was run 15 miles north to Scotia for turning, because of the absence of the necessary facilities at Huntsville. Anyone who wished could remain on board, and the two Northerns pulled away from Huntsville with a far from empty train. The triangular layout at Scotia is formed by two tightly curved connections to the Kearney branch. It had rained, everything was dripping wet and the air was absolutely still. Three attempts were needed to get the 18-car train reversed round the tight curve under those conditions on a rising gradient.

After two tries with the engines losing their feet completely, there was probably enough sand on the rails to make slipping inexcusable and the third attempt was successful and audibly marvellous. The stacatto bark of 6218 and the slightly softer note of 6167 fairly raised the echoes as they propelled nearly 1500 tons of train round the north leg of the wye.

25:
Earlier on 26 September 1964, the two 4-8-4s are seen drawing into Washago, 89 miles north of Toronto.

The sight of Northerns double-heading was extremely rare and almost unbelievable in the virtually steamless days of 1964. So this was indeed a very special occasion — a bitter-sweet time of coming and going.

As 1964 wore on, those who knew CN 6167 well had been aware that her boiler certificate would expire on 30 September that year. Realizing this, CN had with commendable foresight in 1963 rebuilt a similar engine of Class U-2-g, 6218, to take over excursion duties. It was logical that a "last run" for 6167 should take place. The Upper Canada Railway Society decided, with the concurrence of CN, not only to arrange this but to combine it with the introduction of 6218. A two-day week-end with the two Northerns double-heading was therefore organized — the Saturday run to Huntsville and one to Brantford, Paris and Hamilton on the Sunday, both starting from Toronto.

The "new" engine was given the honour of leading for the outward leg of her first run, while for the return portion and the whole of the Sunday excursion 6167 was fittingly given the leading position.

26:
Excursion trains sometimes get to the strangest places. This location in Ferguson Avenue, Hamilton, Ontario where the line to Caledonia runs up the middle of the street, is hardly conducive to high speed running and on this occasion on 23 January 1966 CN 6218 found the speed limit of 5 mph (for trains) virtually unattainable because of a heavy snowfall the previous night. Being a Sunday morning the plows were not out too early! Only the supreme skill of the engineman avoided stalling on the rising gradient. In Toronto, the departure point, 17" of snow fell and many passengers had considerable difficulty in getting to the station. A steam locomotive in an otherwise steamless country provides much incentive, however, and the train was well filled. In fact many enthusiasts at the end of the day felt it had been one of the best trips ever, perhaps because of the adversity. Photographers were often hip deep in snow drifts at runpast locations!

27:
Another 23 January 1966 scene, as CN 6218 is coaled at Paris Junction, Ontario, at the turning point of this 150 mile run from Toronto organized by the Upper Canada Railway Society (UCRS). Behind the big 4-8-4 is the concrete coaling tower, its functioning days long since over. Its replacement in the excursion era is in this instance a CN crane with a clam bucket and a pre-arranged strategically spotted gondola of coal.

28-a:
Obviously this is not a unique picture of CN 6218 on 14 February 1970. It is however an example of the splendid smoke and steam effects that help to make winter excursions so very memorable. The location is Lefroy on the Newmarket Subdivision and the train is a special from Toronto to Barrie, Ontario, for the annual Winter Carnival. Run by the Toronto Train Trip Association, the train continued forward to Orillia for turning and passengers who preferred additional rail mileage to fun on the ice could remain on board.

The last vehicle of the train was unusual in that it was a lounge-observation car, Cape Chignecto, chartered privately by some twenty people with the prime purpose of having a surprise birthday party for one of the fellows on the way home.

The car incorporated a kitchen which was intensively used throughout the day. No less than four guitars and a banjo appeared after the cake had been cut and the smooth riding car did some rocking inside on the return journey. Try this for entertaining your friends sometime. Recommended.

28-b:
Two members of the private party after a visit to the cab during turning at Orillia.

29:
With a light load for a 4-8-4, CN 6218 comes up the hill past Ballantyne with a train reminiscent of the short, fast, medium-distance services of the fifties. It is in fact a Montreal-Toronto excursion on 21 July 1968.

The steam locomotive ran on three weekends in that month between Canada's two largest cities for the Upper Canada Railway Society in conjunction with the Illini Railroad Club, as part of a much longer venture by the latter from Chicago to Newfoundland to see the CN narrow gauge system on the island. To fit in with two week-long trips from Chicago, 6218 operated eastwards on 6 July, returning to Toronto on 13 July; Toronto-Montreal again on 14 July and finally westwards as seen in this photograph. The triangular junction providing access to Montreal yard is behind the train.

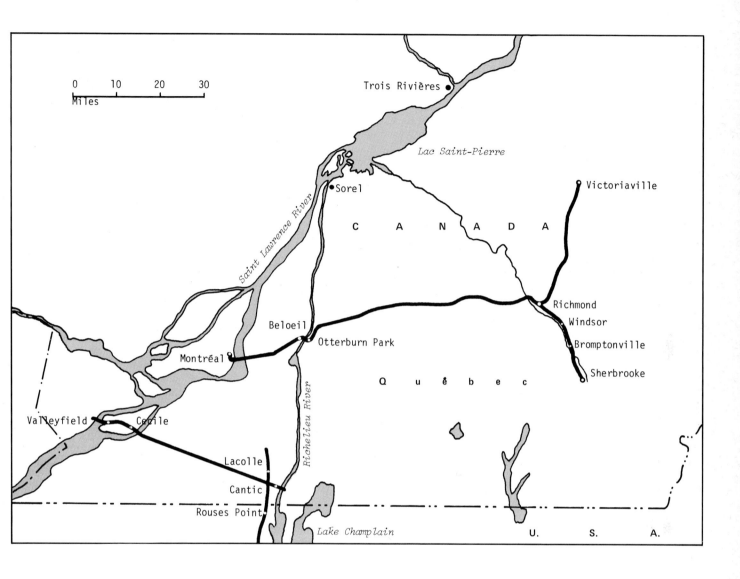

Quebec

Caption to photo appears on page 32.

32:

Mont St. Hilaire provides the background as CN 6218 sets back across the Richelieu River at Beloeil in preparation for a runpast on 21 February 1970. Many of the passengers have detrained at Otterburn Park on the far side of the river, a rather favourite runpast location for trips from Montreal to the Eastern Townships or Quebec via the south shore. The destination on this bitterly cold Sunday was Sherbrooke, Quebec.

Caption to Page 30:

After reaching Richmond, Quebec, on 21 February 1970, CN 6218 proceeded up the valley of the St. Francis River through the paper-making town of Windsor. The temperature was well below zero and a fairly strong wind was blowing, giving promise of good steam effects.

The direction of the low winter sun was ideal and the resulting picture was well worth the freezing forty-minute wait to see 6218 rounding a curve between Windsor and Bromptonville. It is probably significant that, despite easy access from the adjacent road, there was not another soul to be seen on the line at this point!

6218's FAREWELL

34-a:
CN 6218 was withdrawn from excursion service in 1971. To mark the occasion, CN arranged for two days of running on 3 and 4 July between Belleville and Anson Junction, Ontario, a distance of 20 miles which permitted five round trips on the Saturday and two on the Sunday afternoon.

For the last Saturday run careful selection of viewpoint was necessary to make use of the remaining minutes of sunlight and the moon was already high as 6218 gathered speed east of Stirling on the way back to Belleville.

34-b:
CN 6218 alongside the sand tower at Belleville motive power depot after completion of the public runs on Sunday 4 July 1971. The engine has been cleaned in readiness for the Farewell Ceremony at Belleville station in the afternoon, at which the Mayor of Belleville, two CN Vice Presidents and the railway's Area Manager officiated. Townspeople were present in large numbers along with visitors. A fitting conclusion to the proceedings was a most poignant eulogy by Omer Lavallée, well-known Canadian railway historian and author, after which the big Northern made a symbolic and spectacular runpast with three cars.

Caption to Page 33:
On her last revenue-earning run from Belleville on 4 July 1971, CN 6218 reaches the summit at the east end of Stirling, with an immaculate pair of extra flags flying above the marker lamps. During her excursion career every train 6218 hauled was an "extra" (i.e. not regularly scheduled) and she invariably carried the white flags. Smoke deflectors, with which the locomotive had been fitted when built in 1942, were subsequently removed but CN had refitted "elephant ears" for the farewell ceremonies. In October 1973, 6218 was presented by CN to Fort Erie, Ontario — for static display in that city.

U.S.A.

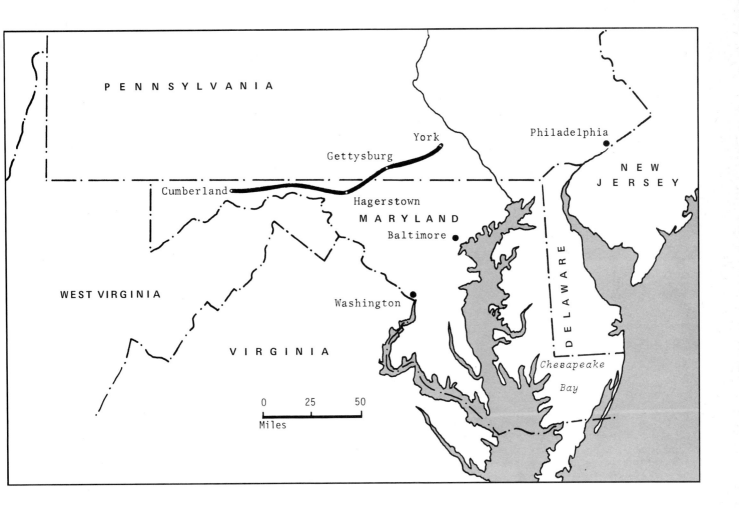

36:
A US engine in Canada. The preserved Reading Railroad 4-8-4 2102 posing as D&H 302 leaves Montreal on 29 April 1973 with a special for Albany, New York. This massive engine took the 22-car train out of CP Rail's Windsor Station and up the climb to Westmount without a trace of slipping.

In April 1973 the Delaware and Hudson Railway celebrated the 150th anniversary of its formation as the Delaware and Hudson Railway and Canal Company. A two-day steam-hauled excursion was arranged to commemorate the event, to run from Colonie, near Albany the company headquarters, to Montreal, the most northerly point served, and reached by running powers over CP Rail tracks. The northbound run was made on 28 April and the return the following day. No D&H steam power was available, hence the use of the Reading engine. In addition, double-heading was required northbound

between Port Henry and Rouses Point, New York, because of severe gradients along the shore of Lake Champlain and an ex-CPR Class G-5 Pacific was obtained from Steamtown, Vermont. It was repainted in D&H livery, re-numbered 653 and fitted with smoke deflectors to complete the D&H "image".

37-b:
It is unlikely that the farmers south of Lacolle, Quebec, would appreciate this type of crop-dusting on 29 April 1973 as Reading 2102 (alias D&H 302) hurries towards the US border in a strong crosswind with the 150th Anniversary excursion returning to Albany, New York.

37-a:
The second tender is clearly seen as the 4-8-4, now back in New York State, accelerates its train of over 1700 tons away from a runpast south of Rouses Point.

38:
In contrast to the glorious weather of the previous day, Sunday 23 October 1966 turned out miserably dull with occasional light drizzle. This did not detract from the interest in the yard at York, Pa. as ex-CPR 972 and ex-Reading 0-6-0 ST 1251 prepared to double-head a rail tour on the "Ma and Pa" — the Maryland and Pennsylvania Railroad — to Delta, Pa. 972 was booked to handle the train alone but the need for additional cars provided an unexpected pairing. Although not visible in this view, the saddletank was equipped with a tender at least as large as that of the 4-6-0.

39:
It might have been in Canada. It was in fact in the State of Pennsylvania in 1966, when a steam weekend was arranged by Rail Tours Inc., an organization founded by George M. Hart, owner of the locomotives pictured here. On 22 October, an excursion was run from York, Pa., the Rail Tours headquarters, to Cumberland, Md., with ex-Canadian Pacific Class G-5-d 4-6-2 1286 and Class D-10-j 4-6-0 972 of the same origin handling the 8-car train over the metals of the Western Maryland Railway.

West of Gettysburg, Pa., the stiff climb up Jack's Mountain has a horse-shoe curve in it and this is the setting for the two emigrants as they battle towards the summit on a crisp autumn morning.

40:
A few British locomotives have ventured across the Atlantic from time to time and for vastly different reasons. King George V, a new four-cylinder 4-6-0 of the Great Western Railway represented Britain at the centenary celebrations of the Baltimore and Ohio Railroad in 1927. The London, Midland and Scottish Railway's Royal Scot, of the same wheel arrangement, came to Canada and the US in 1933. The same company's Duchess of Hamilton 4-6-2 (carrying the name Coronation) toured the US in 1939 and was exhibited at the New York World's Fair. Due to the outbreak of hostilities in Europe, the locomotive was trapped in the US until 1943 and the train was not shipped back to England until 1946. The most recent visitor was ex-London and North Eastern Railway 4-6-2 Flying Scotsman, the first steam locomotive to travel at an authenticated 100 mph, which, like Royal Scot visited both the US and Canada.

In 1969, Flying Scotsman toured the eastern US with a British Trade Mission exhibition train which included two Pullmans and an observation car. The author and a friend took a three-day holiday involving 2361 miles of driving from Montreal as far south as the Carolinas and Georgia to spend just one day following 4472 from Salisbury N.C. to Gainesville, Ga. Nearing the end of that run on 29 October 1969, Flying Scotsman storms up a long Southern Railway grade towards Cornelia, Ga., at a steady 30 mph or so, demonstrating the fact that an A3 Pacific was never designed to run on soft coal.

41:
In 1970, Flying Scotsman came to Canada after wintering in Texas. Port of entry was Sarnia, Ontario, which meant that the apple-green Pacific first set wheel on Canadian rails underground and also underwater! The line crossing the international boundary here is carried under the St. Clair River in a single line tunnel built in 1890.

After being on view in Toronto and Ottawa, Flying Scotsman spent ten days in Montreal, then returned westwards to Kingston and Toronto. This 28 October 1970 photograph by Patricia Bowman, the author's wife, shows the Pacific 28 miles west of Montreal

gathering speed towards Cedars after the three-mile climb from Dorion which culminates in a mile at 1% (1 in 100). The apparently four track section here is actually double track main line flanked by two long sidings, all CTC equipped for bi-directional running.

Flying Scotsman carries the bell presented by the Southern Railway System in 1969 and, mounted on the right side of the smokebox, the whistle from the same US railway company. This was the third, and last, whistle fitted to 4472 during its sojourn in North America. The engine's own LNER whistle — the piercing high-pitched one — was retained and was used frequently.

42:
Bound for Victoriaville on 15 September 1973, CN 6060 barks away crisply up the hill towards St. Hilaire East after the double runpast at Otterburn Park.

All but three classes of CN steam locomotives were painted overall black. The U-1-f was one of the exceptions with black boiler cladding, frames, cylinders and running gear contrasting pleasantly with green cab, running board skirts and Vanderbilt tender. 6060 was coal-fired when built, but is now oil-fired. Photograph by Patricia Bowman.

43:
Seen from the right bank of the Richelieu River, Class U-1-f 4-8-2 CN 6060 takes a runpast across the bridge between Beloeil and Otterburn Park on 15 September 1973. This was the locomotive's first public run since restoration, the train was full and vantage points such as this were busy. 6060 crossed this bridge no less than six times on the trip! First on arrival from Montreal to detrain passengers who wished to photograph the two runpasts, which themselves accounted for four more crossings, and finally on the homeward journey in the evening. The owner of this river-front property is apparently quite amenable to occasional invasions of his back garden. It happens every time an excursion passes this way!

These photographs are on the next two pages:

44:

During the summers of 1973 and 1974, the National Capital Commission in Ottawa chartered Ontario Rail Association equipment for Sunday excursions and also for special events such as the Maxville Highland Games. These runs have proved to be very popular, requiring early booking to be sure of a seat. On occasion this meant in the first two hours after the tickets went on sale on the Monday prior to each weekly trip.

In 1974, the chosen destination was Wakefield, Quebec, on the CP Rail Maniwaki Subdivision. The line traverses the valley of the Gatineau River, a glimpse of which can be seen just ahead of the engine as 1057 heads southwards near Cascades with the return inaugural excursion on 30 June.

The business car next to the locomotive is "Mount Stephen", a former directors' car built at the CP Rail Angus Shops in 1926 and named after Lord Mount

Stephen, the first president of the Canadian Pacific Railway Company. The elegant interior is finished in inlaid Circassian walnut. This very heavy car which turns the scales at just over 101 tons is now assigned to Canadian Pacific's Public Relations and Advertising Department and forms part of the company's display train.

45:

With safety valves hissing furiously, 1057 pauses prior to a runpast near Elmira, Ontario, on 6 April 1974. Elmira is renowned for its annual maple syrup festival and 1057, an ex-Canadian Pacific class D-10-h 4-6-0 now in the care of the Ontario Rail Association, made the run from West Toronto with eight cars of steam — and syrup — enthusiasts especially for this event.

The lettering "Credit Valley" is in anticipation of the day when the Ontario Rail Association will operate its own line, presently the CN Beeton Subdivision running north from Georgetown, which follows the course of the Credit River.

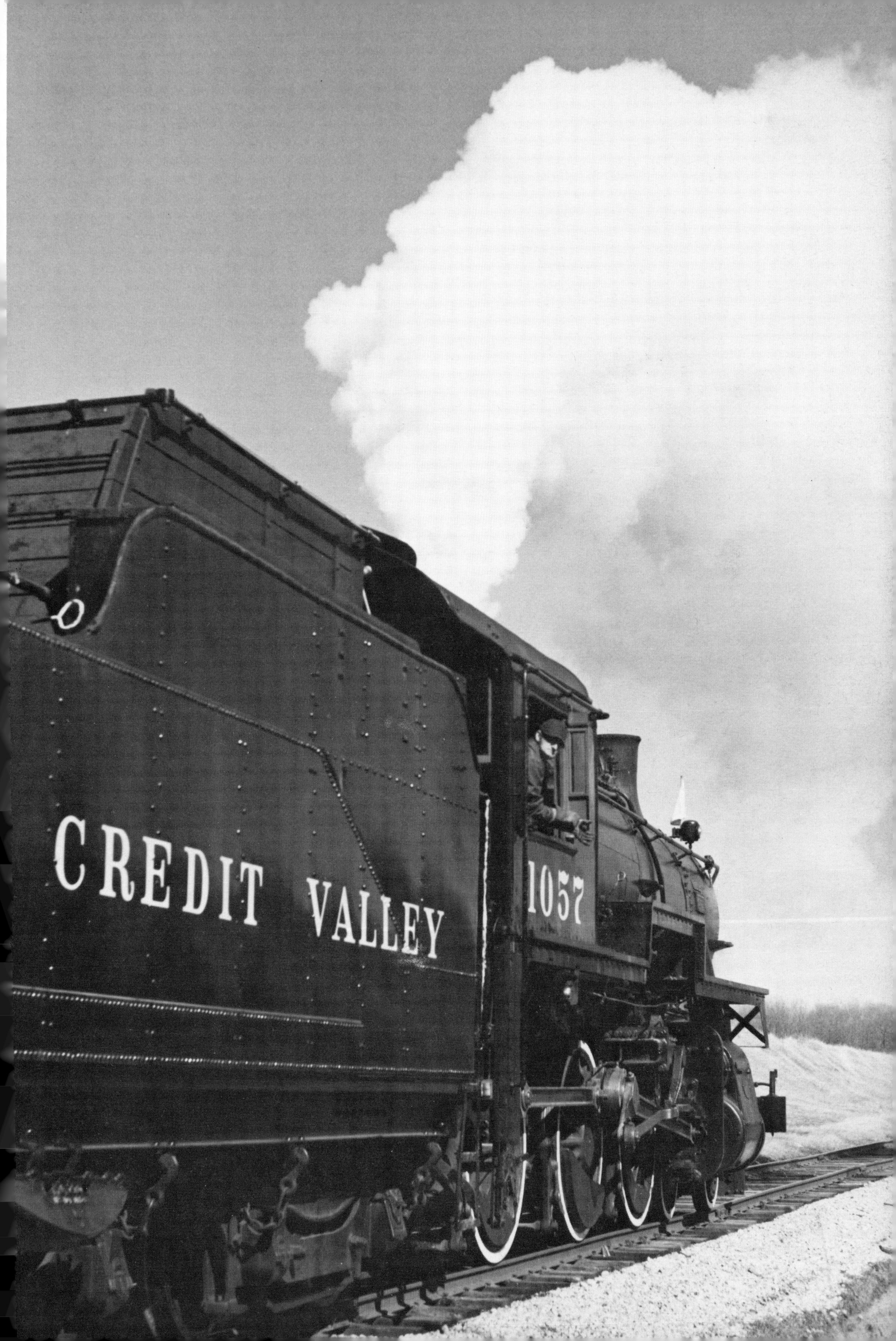
CREDIT VALLEY
1057

46:
Ontario Rail Association locomotives operated double-headed on three occasions in May 1974. Here 4-4-0 136 and 4-6-0 1057 descend from the heights of the Niagara escarpment between Waterdown and Hamilton Junction on the Goderich Subdivision on 4 May 1974.

The Association has received a great deal of cooperation from CP Rail. Space and technical assistance has been provided at the John Street roundhouse in Toronto for restoration, housing and maintenance of the locomotives; train crews are provided at prevailing rates; and runpasts are permitted on main lines as well as on branch and secondary lines, all of which adds up to a major contribution to the enjoyment of many enthusiasts and others for whom the steam engine is a reminder of a past era.

47:
Earlier on 4 May 1974, the vintage pair climb the escarpment towards Campbellville on the double-track Galt Subdivision en route from West Toronto to Hamilton via Guelph Junction.

The locomotives, both of Canadian Pacific origin, are of considerable age, 136 having been built in 1883 and 1057 in 1912. In 1973 136, a class A-2-m engine, took part in a television production by the Canadian Broadcasting Corporation of "The National Dream", a serialization of the historical events leading up to the formation of the CPR and the construction of that company's line across Canada. For the film sequences the engine carried various numbers and in some scenes appeared with a diamond stack, a common feature of locomotives of the period.

48:
Nearing their destination on 4 May 1974 136 and 1057 drift down towards lake level by the inner part of Hamilton harbour.

3 | ENGLAND

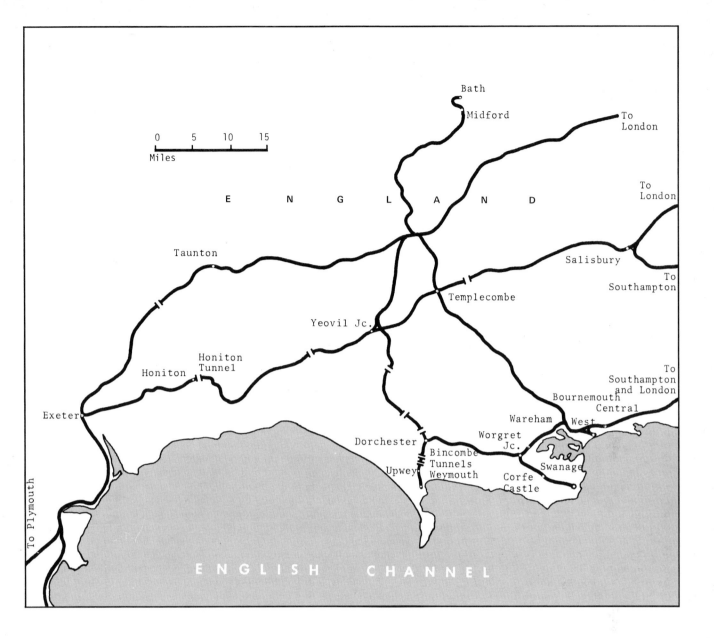

Southern England

50:
A rather short, first visit to London meant trying to see as many of the main line termini as possible. Strange that places like King's Cross, Marylebone, St. Pancras and Victoria seemed so familiar before ever having been there. In 1963, Saturday still seemed to be the day that most Englishmen started and finished holidays judging by the number of special trains being run out of the ex-London and South Western Railway terminus at Waterloo on 15 June.

A small boy gazes intently from a carriage window as 34095 Brentor pulls away with an express for the Exeter line. This is a rebuilt example of the West Country class 3-cylinder Pacifics designed by Bulleid for the Southern Railway and introduced in 1945. Originally the class was streamlined (air-smoothed was the term used) and equipped with Bulleid's unusual chain driven valve gear encased in an oil bath. In 1957, rebuilding began, and more than half of the class lost their air-amoothed casings and were fitted with Walschaerts gear before BR called a halt because of the decision to eliminate steam. Many of the later engines carried commemorative names and were known as the Battle of Britain class, but otherwise they were identical to the West Countries.

52:
A Battle of Britain Pacific in original form. 34051 Winston Churchill streaks down Honiton bank with the 1520 Exeter Central to Templecombe passenger on 17 June 1963. This location was chosen primarily to photograph and record trains coming from the opposite direction, when they had been climbing for six miles, mostly at 1 in 80. There was therefore a tendency to concentrate on sound and the uphill pictures that were taken proved to be less interesting than this one.

34051 was condemned, but had not been cut up when the wartime leader died. The 4-6-2 was promptly refurbished and returned to service to haul Sir Winston's funeral train from Waterloo to Handborough in Oxfordshire on 30 January 1965. Quite unwittingly the great statesman had extended the working life of the Pacific named after him.

53:
West Country class Pacific 34004 Yeovil gets the road at Dorchester South on 18 May 1966. This station was for many years rather unique, in that the double track line had a platform for the Weymouth direction only. The Bournemouth/London platform was on a short spur, so trains from Weymouth had to run past the switch and propel back into the platform – an awkward operating problem which was corrected a few years ago by construction of a new "up" platform on the main line.

Looking carefully at the sign "Passengers must . . . ." would suggest that the railways are rather thrifty organizations. The white letters S.R. denote Southern Region, or, in the days before nationalization on 1 January 1948, Southern Railway. The spacing is rather odd and close inspection reveals the letters L & SWR cast on the sign – London and South Western Railway, which ceased to exist on 1 January 1923!!!

54:
Somerset is one of the loveliest of English counties, Bath is one of the most delightful places in the county, and running generally southwards and eastwards from this city the Somerset and Dorset Joint Railway wound its way over the Mendip Hills and through Blackmoor Vale to Bournemouth. This line was a venture of two of the pre-grouping companies, the Midland and the LSWR, and even after the 1923 Grouping continued to be jointly owned by the LMS and the Southern. Even in BR days it was inter-regional and provided one of the few through routes from the north of England to the south coast which avoided London.

A few miles south of Bath is the village of Midford which provides in a small area a good variety of vantage points. The morning of 18 June 1963 was disappointingly misty, but, in being so, offered a greater challenge for the photographer. Contrast — or lack of it — being the main problem, the south end of the tiny, single-platform station enabled the steam to be set off against the far side of the valley, as BR Standard Class 5 4-6-0 73049 came off the single track section with the 0953 Bath (Green Park) to Bournemouth West.

55:
After the early mist on 18 June 1963, a short period of heavy rain cleared the air and only half an hour after 73049 went south, sister engine 73052 barked away from the Midford stop with the 0905 Templecombe to Bath (Green Park) in clear, bright conditions. Wild flowers in profusion added a touch of colour to the steep cutting sides.

Although the locomotive is one of the BR Standard designs, the coaches are still typically Southern, even to the extent of retaining that company's green livery when the other regions of BR were uniformly maroon.

57: *(opposite)*

Half-way down the Swanage branch lies the picturesque village of Corfe Castle. The ruins of the castle itself are a prominent landmark and, being open to the public for a small charge, also provide a fine viewpoint for photography.

In the nineteen sixties, some ex-LMS tank locomotives were drafted to the Southern Region. One of the strangers, an Ivatt Class 2 2-6-2T brings the 1025 Wareham (the main line station) to Swanage into Corfe Castle on 18 May 1966, with the ruins on the skyline. The branch is single with a passing loop at this station and has been closed for some considerable time. Steps are being taken by the Swanage Railway Society to reopen it as a private venture.

56: *(opposite)*

West of Bournemouth, on the line to Weymouth, port for the Channel Islands, a branch diverges to the seaside resort of Swanage at Worgret Junction, 35007 Aberdeen Commonwealth keeps to the main line on 18 May 1966 with 0830 London (Waterloo) to Weymouth.

The locomotive is a Merchant Navy class 4-6-2, the larger of Bulleid's two Pacific designs. Its 250 psi boiler pressure, three 18" x 24" cylinders and 74" drivers gave it a tractive effort of 33,495 lbs, thus putting it into power classification 8P, the highest BR passenger rating. As the class name might suggest, all 30 engines were called after well known shipping lines. Like Bulleid's West Country and Battle of Britain Pacifics, the Merchant Navies (introduced in 1941) started life with air-smoothed casings and Bulleid valve gear. Rebuilding commenced in 1956 and the whole class was so treated. Two examples have been preserved in England — 35005 Canadian Pacific and 35028 Clan Line. The former is at Steamtown, Carnforth, while Clan Line, owned by the Merchant Navy Locomotive Preservation Society, is based at Ashford, Kent, and is cleared for running on BR lines.

58-a:
The area around the Bincombe Tunnels, a few miles north of Weymouth offers a good deal of viewpoint variety. The short southernmost tunnel takes the trains under the main road while the other, approximately 0.5 mile long, burrows under the high ground south of Dorchester, the county town of Dorset. The relativity of the tunnels is seen in this photograph looking north. Both locomotives are West Country Pacifics; 34098 on the right (appropriately named Weymouth) and 34101 Hartland emerging from the longer tunnel. The picture was taken from the long-since closed but delightfully named Upwey Wishing Well Halt.

58-b:
Between the tunnels, 34098 Weymouth streaks down the hill towards its namesake destination with the 1030 from Waterloo on 11 June 1966.

59:
From above the south portal of the short tunnel, trains can be seen winding up the climb from Weymouth, working hard on the 1 in 50 (2%) gradient.

A stiff breeze weaves the exhaust into intricate patterns on 11 June 1966 as Merchant Navy class 35026 Lamport & Holt Line approaches the Bincombe Tunnels with the 1125 Weymouth to Waterloo.

60:
The same engine and the same train as that on the previous page, photographed from exactly the same position. Alas, steam had vanished before all the potential of this location could be exploited.

Western England

61:
No. 76031 with the 1647 Weymouth-Bournemouth train near Upwey on 18 May 1966.

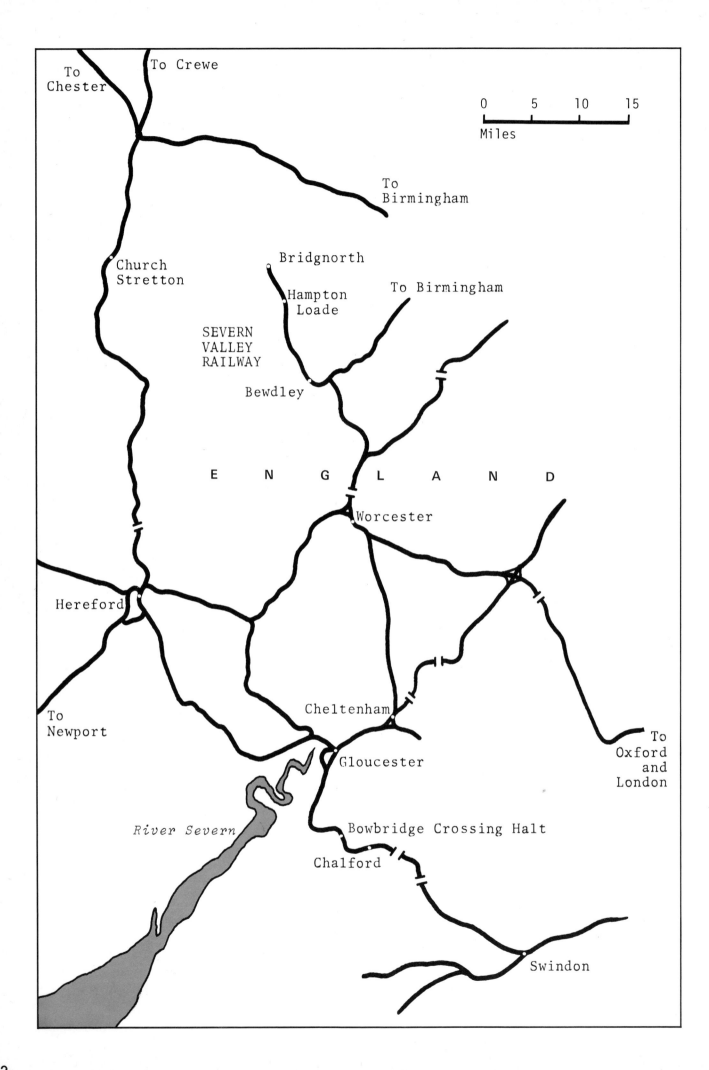

63:
Typical of the branch line or local cross-country service was the 1930 to Hereford seen gathering speed on the outskirts of Gloucester on 18 June 1963, and hauled by one of the ubiquitous 2-6-2Ts of the former Great Western Railway.

The "inevitable" van was also very typical. Any urgent or perishable traffic on lightly travelled lines was often taken by the next passenger train, sometimes on the tail end and frequently "inside the engine". Such commodities as fish, flowers and soft fruits were carried in this way to be picked up or set off at some quiet country station or taken through to the next major town or junction from which the van could be forwarded in a fast freight or parcels train.

The picture was in no way planned. The train was seen at Gloucester Central about to depart with no good viewpoint quickly attainable. Using sense of direction and every ounce of the car's acceleration (it was a first visit to the area) a quick dash to the edge of the town was amply rewarded. There was just enough time to stop the car and couple on a telephoto lens to capture this rural service on a fine summer evening.

64:
Great Western 4-6-0s at Worcester Shrub Hill 19 June 1963. The Hall class on the left has just arrived with the Hereford portion of a London (Paddington) train (extreme left) and, using the scissors crossover mid-way along the platform, has coupled off with a bogie van. 7025 Sudeley Castle already waiting at the south end of the platform with several additional coaches, prepares to back down and couple on to those originating in Hereford, the combined train going forward as the 1310 to Paddington.

Sudeley Castle was one of the later examples of its class of 171 engines built between 1923 and 1950. The first withdrawal took place five months before the final Castle entered service! There were detail differences within the class, such as 3- or 4-row superheaters and some double chimneys, but all had four 16" x 26" cylinders, inside Walschaerts valve gear, 225psi boiler pressure and 80.5" coupled wheels.

65:
A visit to Banbury mpd on 20 May 1966 really produced the unexpected. All the Castles had been withdrawn by this time and it was a great surprise to find 7029 Clun Castle in steam, but the Shedmaster explained the situation. The locomotive had been purchased privately and Banbury was doing maintenance work on behalf of its new owner. 7029 took a dead locomotive to Tyseley (Birmingham) for repair later in the day, thereby combining a test run with some useful work for BR. Clun Castle was one of the members of the class fitted with a four-row superheater and now fully restored it is in the care of the Standard Gauge Steam Trust at Tyseley.

66:
Grazing cattle seem to be the only spectators but this was far from the case as 6000 King George V and 4472 Flying Scotsman accelerated away from Church Stretton on 22 September 1973. There were indeed dozens of people at this point (some hidden by the steam!) and hundreds all along the route of the Atlantic Venturers Express, which ran from Plymouth to Shrewsbury and return, with 6000 and 4472 working 15 coaches northbound between Newport and Shrewsbury, where the train was divided. 6000 took the return portion to Newport, while 4472 continued north for a two-week tour. Flying Scotsman won the toss by the Mayor of Newport and led as far as Hereford where the engines changed positions.

The train was so named because the locomotives, as mentioned in Section 2, had both crossed the Atlantic. Both carry the bells presented to them in the US.

Flying Scotsman, privately owned by Mr. A. Pegler for some ten years since withdrawal by BR, is now the property of Mr. W. McAlpine, while King George V was bought by H.P. Bulmer Ltd., the Hereford cider makers. It is cared for on behalf of Bulmer's Cider by the 6000 Locomotive Association at Hereford and, unlike Flying Scotsman, retains its BR livery.

67-a:
In absolutely immaculate condition, King George V climbs towards Church Stretton on 22 September 1973 with the 11-coach southbound Atlantic Venturers Express. Again there were many people around but it was still possible to obtain a photograph in which none of them appeared. The deep note of the King's exhaust gave evidence of the 1 in 100 (1%) gradient and the fact that the train was nearing the top of thirteen miles of almost unbroken collar work from Shrewsbury.

The Kings were the largest and most powerful 4-6-0s of the Great Western Railway and indeed, of all British 4-6-0s. Like the Castles they had four cylinders, but the Kings' were bigger, 16.25" x 28". The 250 psi pressure and 78" drivers gave a tractive effort of 40,285 lbs, figures identical to those of the London, Midland and Scottish Princess Royal 4-6-2s introduced in 1933. Stanier, their designer, was Chief Mechanical Engineer of the LMS from 1932 to 1944, but prior to that he was a Great Western man. Significant? In terms of tractive effort, only the Class A2 Pacific of the LNER was more powerful and that only marginally.

67-b:
Awaiting King George V on one of the little roads leading to All Stretton. XOK 480 has not parked. All others have!!

68:
A type of locomotive usually associated with the Great Western Railway was the pannier tank, of which the company owned literally hundreds. Some were even built in the early days of BR and several, of different classes, are now in use on operating lines owned by preservation societies. One of these is the Severn Valley Railway in Shropshire. Leaving the northern end of the line at Bridgnorth with the 1815 to Hampton Loade is 0-6-OPT 5764 of the ex-GWR 5700 class. Built in June 1929 at Swindon, this engine served the GWR and BR until May 1960 when it was withdrawn, shopped at Swindon, and bought by London Transport. Carrying their number L95, it was used on permanent way and engineers' trains, usually after dark. Now owned by the Pannier Tank Fund it has been restored to Great Western livery.

69:
Short distance and branch line services of the GWR were often worked on the push-pull principle. A common engine for these "auto-trains", as they were known, was the 0-4-2T of the 1400 class, a Collett design for light branch work weighing a little over 41 tons.

On 29 April 1964, 1451 leaves Bowbridge Crossing Halt with the 0930 Chalford — Gloucester Central, a main line local service. The auto-trailers were fitted with driving cabs. Controls could be transmitted through two trailers, but no more, because of the physical effort required by the driver to operate the entirely mechanical system. A three or four coach auto-train could be operated by marshalling the locomotive in the centre in which case it was operated from a driving cab in both directions. This system is in use today on the preserved Dart Valley Railway in Devon.

70-a:
The stark solidity of steel contrasts with the ethereal undulations of the moors as a train of limestone coasts down the 1 in 100 at Ribblehead behind a BR Standard class 9F 2-10-0. The location is on the Settle and Carlisle line of the Midland Railway, later LMSR.

70-b:
A few miles down the line at Horton-in-Ribblesdale, a BR Standard class 4 4-6-0 shunts the yard, with what appears to be a supply for the local pub in the wagon. Perhaps they were only empties! Both photographs were taken on 23 May 1966.

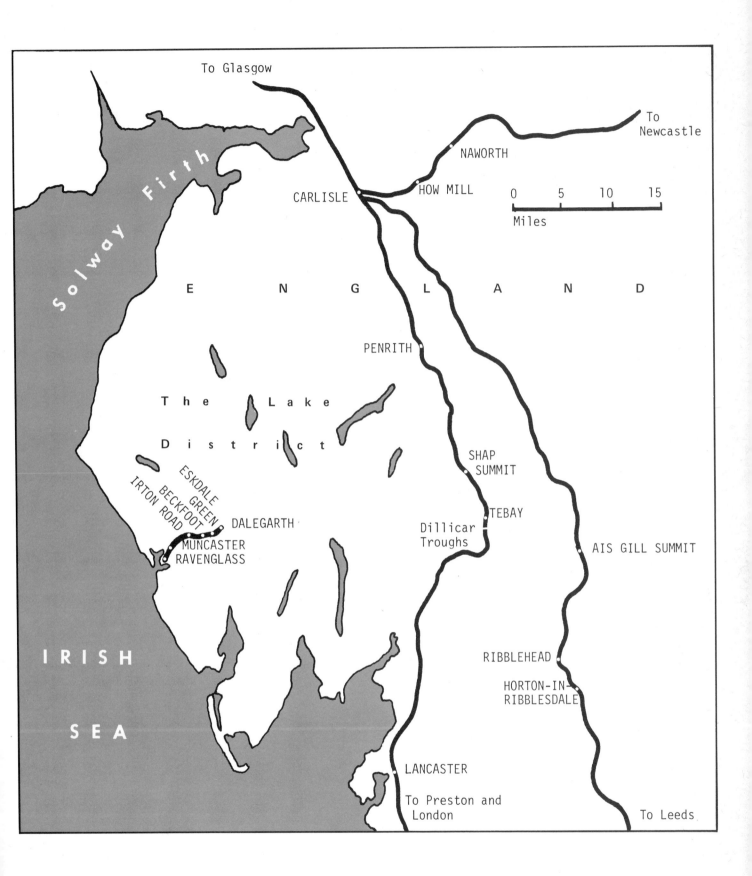

To Glasgow

To Newcastle

NAWORTH

CARLISLE

HOW MILL

0   5   10   15
Miles

Solway Firth

E   N   G   L   A   N   D

PENRITH

The   Lake

District

SHAP
SUMMIT

ESKDALE
GREEN
BECKFOOT
IRTON ROAD

DALEGARTH

TEBAY

Dillicar
Troughs

MUNCASTER
RAVENGLASS

AIS GILL SUMMIT

IRISH

RIBBLEHEAD

HORTON-IN-
RIBBLESDALE

SEA

LANCASTER

To Preston and
London

To Leeds

The North-West

Ais Gill —
highest main
line summit
in England.

72-a:
Approaching Ais Gill with stone from Long Meg quarry, class 9F 92161 breasts the summit of the gruelling climb from the north, uphill most of the 48 miles from Carlisle. Eleven of the last fifteen miles are at 1 in 100 (1%). The engine is one of the Standard 2-10-0s introduced by BR as late as 1954 of which 251 were built. It is sad that the working life of such fine machines was so short — all had been withdrawn by 1968 — but fortunately two have been preserved in operating condition for posterity; 92203, given the name Black Prince by its owner Mr. David Shepherd, the wildlife and railway artist; and 92220 Evening Star by BR. Presently on loan to the Keighley and Worth Valley Railway, the latter engine was the last new steam locomotive built by BR.

72-b:
A Stanier class 8F 2-8-0 passes Ais Gill box with a northbound freight on 23 May 1966. The elevation is 1100 feet above sea level at the boundary between the counties of Westmorland and Yorkshire and the official summit board is visible at the extreme left of the picture. The summit is actually a short level stretch a little over half a mile long.

73:
One of the most successful British steam designs was the class 5MT introduced by William Stanier (later Sir William) of the LMS in 1934 — the Black Fives as they became affectionately known. Construction continued during and after World War II. There were eventually 842 of them. In BR days, they penetrated to most parts of the system and were still active in the last days of BR standard gauge steam, outlasting many newer engines of later design. This versatile 72-ton 4-6-0 was equally at home on passenger and freight work and the MT (mixed traffic) designation was never more appropriately applied.

Wild Boar Fell provides the background as 45274 fights its way up to Ais Gill in the teeth of a gale with a load of structural steel on 23 May 1966.

74:
On the West Coast main line, there used to be a set of water troughs or track pans at Dillicar in the Lune Gorge just south of Tebay. One of the later series of Black Fives replenishes its tender tank while the safety valves show a full head of steam ready for the assault on the 1 in 75 of Shap bank, just a short distance ahead.

44767 was unique in being the only Black Five fitted with Stephenson link motion (experimentally in 1947) in place of the usual Walschaerts valve gear. Several other post-war members of the class were Caprotti equipped.

75-a:
With just a trace of grey haze from the chimney Class 9F 92012 heads north over the troughs at the head of a trainload of bridge girders which had a brake van at each end. This viewpoint was very accessible by quiet rural roads, but now the troughs have gone, catenary marches along the line and a new motorway slashes the hillside above — a great change from 1966.

75-b:
Creating a considerable tail wave, another Black Five streaks over the troughs with the scoop clearly visible. The boiler appears to have been in use as a pigeon roost!

A gem of the north-west
— the Ravenglass and Eskdale.

On the west coast of Cumberland is an unusual estuary — a triple one which, on the map, is beginning to look like an octopus. The three rivers are the Irt, the Mite and the Esk, the last of which gives its name to a fine narrow gauge railway — the Ravenglass and Eskdale. Originally built in 1875 as a three foot gauge line, it was converted to fifteen inches in 1915-17. Ravenglass, the western terminus, is situated on the estuary and also has a British Rail station. In addition to providing a useful local service, the line attracts a great deal of tourist traffic to the area, Eskdale itself extending well into the mountains of the very scenic Lake District.

76-a:
Despite its name, the railway does not follow the River Esk all the way. Rather it heads north-eastwards up the valley of the Mite for a few miles before crossing into Eskdale. In this 14 May 1968 scene at Muncaster the railway's River Esk is mirrored in nature's River Mite, while two ducks paddle upstream.

This picture was preceded by a minor disaster. Insufficient time had been allowed to get into position, thereby necessitating a brisk sprint, but a bit of uneven paving caused a stumble which resulted in one railway photographer lying in a heap on the road. Just for a few seconds, though, and the train was photographed in the desired position as planned. Only then was the damage assessed; a grazed knee, a slightly sprained wrist, a bent lens hood and worst of all, a jacket with a badly ripped sleeve. The camera itself suffered no ill effects, but it was a rather expensive negative.

76-b:
Seen from the footplate, River Irt draws to a halt at Eskdale Green to pick up a passenger and her dog.

77:
After coupling off, turning and running round, 0-8-2 River Irt waits on the centre road at Ravenglass while 2-8-2 River Esk backs down in readiness for the next departure to Dalegarth. A third engine, as might be expected, is named River Mite.

78:
The single-manned locomotives of the R & ER burn coke. The seat on the front of the tender has just enough room for two people and the author was privileged to occupy one half on River Irt at the kind invitation of the driver.

Here River Esk, in lined black livery, departs from Beckfoot with the 1215 Dalegarth — Ravenglass on 14 May 1968.

79:
As at Ravenglass, a turntable is provided at Dalegarth, the eastern end of the line. With the rugged Lakeland fells in the background a cheerful driver and guard give 0-8-2 River Irt a rather nonchalant push round. There is no unnecessary trackwork here as the turntable itself gives the engine access to the runround loop. River Irt is finished in apple green reminiscent of the LNER and lined out in black and white.

80:
Late in September 1973, Flying Scotsman set off on a tour of the north of England with the Bulmer's Cider Exhibition Train, visiting a number of major cities at which the train was open to the public. Owned by H.P. Bulmer Ltd., it consists of Pullman cars Aquila, Christine, Eve, Prinia and Morella fitted out respectively as lounge, standard Pullman seating, the bar, exhibit car (displays and models of cider-making equipment) and film projection car.

On 4 October 1973, Flying Scotsman storms up the 1 in 107 past How Mill en route from Carlisle to Newcastle with the Cider Express.

81-a:
Saturday 6 October 1973 saw another preserved LNER Pacific operating two round trips between Newcastle and Carlisle — Class A4 4498 Sir Nigel Gresley. Fully restored to the unique garter blue livery used by the LNER exclusively for the A4s, 4498 is owned by the A4 Locomotive Society which ran one of the two excursions, named The Hadrian because the line runs close to Hadrian's Wall, a famous relic of Roman times. A foggy morning dictated the viewpoint to a certain extent, as there were some areas where the fog was very dense. Steam has just been shut off near Naworth as 4498 starts the descent from the Northumberland moors down through How Mill to Carlisle.

81-b:
Just a few seconds earlier 4498 was seen in rather different perspective from the same viewpoint through a most useful zoom lens.

82:
Fife is that peninsular county of Scotland lying
between the estuaries of the Forth and Tay, whose
famous bridges provide the principal rail links to
south and north respectively. The western part of the
county is noted for its coal mining, the north and east
are rich farming areas, there is a sizeable paper-
making industry and fishing is carried on along the
coast. The main line of the North British Railway
(later LNER and BR) from Edinburgh to Dundee and
Aberdeen cuts across the peninsula, but there used to
be another way to Dundee — the circuitous coastal

route from Thornton Junction to Leuchars Junction
serving the fishing burghs, the farming communities
and the university town of St. Andrews.

Pittenweem was the starting point of the author's
first journey by rail. The train would have been
hauled, in all probability, by one of W.P. Reid's Scott
or Glen class 4-4-0s which were the dominant
passenger power at the time and for some twenty
years afterwards. They were eventually ousted by the
LNER class B1 4-6-0, one of which is seen from the
goods loading bank in this 30 May 1966 scene.
Passenger services had been withdrawn the year
before. 61308 is arriving from the west with the
single daily goods service a few months before the
East Fife line was closed entirely.

SCOTLAND

85:
Diminutive and delightful is probably the best description of British Aluminium Company 0-4-0ST 3. This little Andrew Barclay engine of 1937 is seen shunting at the company's Burntisland works on a fine afternoon in May 1968. The locomotive depot can be seen in this picture just above the wagon next to the engine.

84:
Its duties for the day completed BAC 3 comes up the hill to the depot where its mates are already "on shed", one under repair and the other in steam.

86:
The British Aluminum Company was very willing to allow visitors to photograph its three steam locomotives (at that time; one has since gone to the Lochty Private Railway) with the proviso that an escort had to be provided. When the author arrived, all work had been finished for the day but the crew of No. 3 did not hesitate for a moment to couple up a few wagons and put on a show.

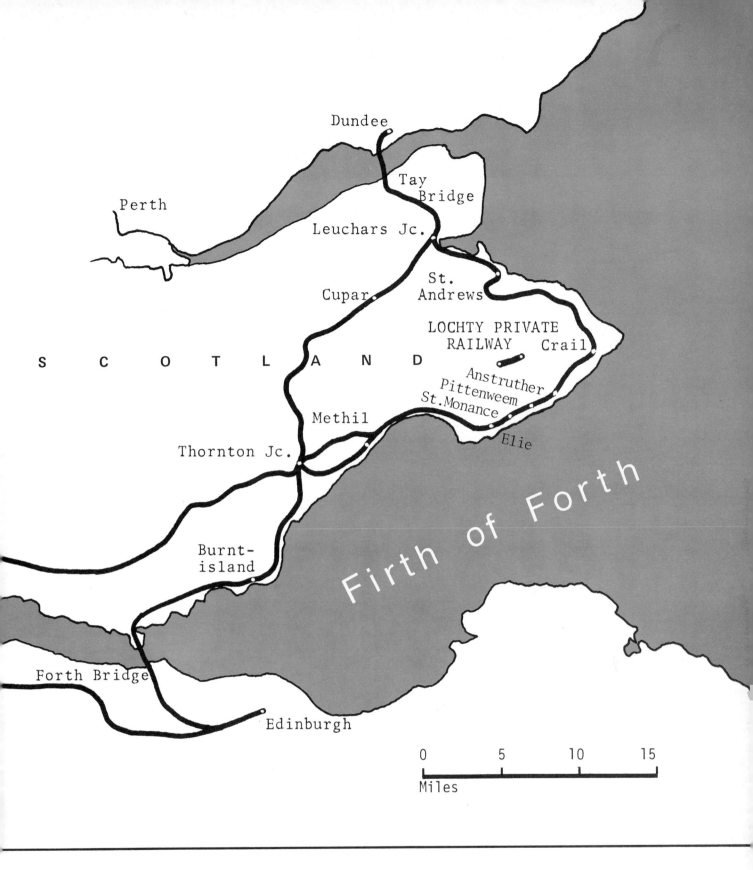

The East Fife Line

— where it all began

88:
Originally the East Fife "loop" was two separate branches — Leuchars to St. Andrews and Thornton to Anstruther. The link between the termini was completed on 1 June 1887 and the original stations were relegated to goods traffic, new through ones having been built to replace them.

On a blustery day in 1963, the old platforms and engine shed are still very much in evidence as the B1-hauled 1230 Crail — Edinburgh (Waverley) changes tablets with the Anstruther signalman. The "new" station, now derelict, is just out of the picture to the left. The line was single throughout with passing loops at most of the stations and the electric tablet system was used. The brass tablet, after withdrawal from the signalbox instrument, was put into a leather pouch with hoop to facilitate exchange with trains on the move.

Services from Edinburgh and Glasgow not running through to Dundee usually went as far as Crail, but the only turntable on the line was at Anstruther. Terminating passenger engines therefore had to run back the 4.5 miles to turn. The other B1, 61345, has done just that and waits in the spur prior to returning to Crail to pick up its next working. The turntable can just be seen to the left of the end of the train.

89-a:
If ever a turntable needed vacuum operation, the one at Anstruther was it. It did not work too badly with the ex-NBR 4-4-0s and 0-6-0s but when the heavier B1 4-6-0s took over it became a real backbreaker. The combined wheelbase of a B1 and tender was actually too long but the problem was solved by cantilevering the turntable rails about 2 ft beyond the circumference of the pit at each end. It was a tight fit at that and it was virtually impossible to balance the engine. The enginemen usually got help from the guard and anyone else around and still it needed every ounce of strength they could muster. They were strong men but that turntable had to be pushed almost every inch of the way — no easing off part way and letting the momentum carry the engine round.

The author felt somewhat guilty for not lending a hand on 14 May 1964 as 61103 was being turned.

89-b:
Class B1 4-6-0 61343 with the eastbound Thornton-Crail goods skirts the short of the Firth of Forth between Elie and St. Monance on 28 June 1963. The load is almost entirely household coal. Most stations on the line had a siding used exclusively by the local coal merchants right up until closure.

Captions to photographs appear on page 92.

92:
In the East Neuk of Fife, a short stretch of the Lochty branch has been relaid through the efforts of a local farmer, Mr. John Cameron, and several business associates, and is now known as the Lochty Private Railway. The company's first engine, class A4 Pacific 60009 Union of South Africa, departs from Lochty on 27 June 1971 on one of the runs to Knightsward.

"The Union", built in 1937, is one of five of the streamlined 4-6-2s which were specially prepared for working the LNER Coronation trains between Edinburgh and London. It was moved to Lochty in 1967 and operated summer Sunday services until the end of the 1972 season. Once again permitted to run on BR tracks, this A4 was one of those active on main line excursions in 1973 and 1974, its place at Lochty being taken by two industrial tank engines, one of which, as mentioned earlier, was obtained from the British Aluminium Company Ltd. The other is an ex-Wemyss Private Railway 0-6-0 ST.

93-b:
Mr. Cameron eases Union of South Africa to a stand at the other end of the line as a maintenance crew looks on. There are no runround facilities and trains are therefore propelled back to Lochty.

This locomotive is the first A4 that the author ever set eyes on. As LNER 4488 in Garter blue livery to match its train, it was seen streaking down the 1 in 78 from Edinburgh (Waverley) with the Coronation in 1937, shortly after its introduction. Due to the kindness of Mr. Cameron 60009 also provided the author with his first run in an A4 cab.

Appropriately, the second vehicle of the train is one of the Coronation observation cars which, with their beaver tails modified, saw service on the scenic routes of the West Highlands in the BR era. Another has been preserved by the Gresley Society and is presently on the Keighley and Worth Valley Railway in Yorkshire, England.

Captions to photographs from previous pages:

90:
After cessation of steam services on BR, there was still steam to be seen in Fife at several locations. In fact at the Wellesley Colliery, Methil, the locomotives of two owners could be seen together, and in this 13 May 1968 scene, Wemyss Private Railway 18, a Barclay 0-6-0T, brings a load of coal wagons out of the sidings at Methil en route to the washing plant at Wellesley, while National Coal Board 8, fitted with Giesl ejector, eases up to a signal at danger — appropriately! — on an adjacent track.

91-a:
Lunch-time line-up as the NCB stud at Wellesley has a breather after servicing. They were all 0-6-0Ts but quite a varied group. The two Barclays, 8 and 10, were outwardly similar except for the Giesl ejector fitted to 8, but 19 was a Hunslet saddletank, a powerful inside cylinder engine of the type developed during the war and generally referred to as the Austerity.

91-b:
A closer look at NCB 8 as the char is cleaned out on 6 May 1968. This 0-6-0T was also built at the Caledonia Works of Andrew Barclay in Kilmarnock.

93-a:
Seen from the ferry slip at North Queensferry in the days before the road bridge was opened, ex-LNER class A2 Pacific 60525 A.H. Peppercorn brings the 1725 Edinburgh to Aberdeen off the north cantilever of the Forth Bridge. This unique tubular and lattice structure has central spans formed by three double cantilevers with suspended spans between adjacent pairs and a series of lattice girder viaduct spans at either end. Opened in 1891, its total length is 1 mile 1006 yds, the longest span is 1710 ft and rail level is 158 feet above high water. The painted surfaces of the steelwork amount to 145 acres — a constant maintenance item over the tidal salt water.

The A2s had somewhat interesting origins. The first six were rebuilt in 1943 and 1944 from the Gresley P2 passenger 2-8-2s introduced in 1934 principally for the difficult Aberdeen route. The next four, with detail differences, were to have been the last V2 2-6-2s but they were outshopped in 1944 and 1945 as 4-6-2s. Thompson, Gresley's successor as the LNER Chief Mechanical Engineer, continued production of his first Pacific design with a new batch introduced in 1946. Finally, Peppercorn who in turn took over when Thompson retired, produced a further development with a shorter wheelbase and brought the class total to 40 engines. Like all the ex-LNER Pacifics they were 3-cylinder machines.

94:
The western exit from Waverley Station is flanked on both sides by Princes Street Gardens, located in the heart of the city and beautifully kept by the Parks Department. In those gardens, there are a number of monuments to famous men, but none so impressive as that to Sir Walter Scott (1771-1832) which was completed in 1844. The tower, supported by four arches, rises to 200 ft and beneath it is a white marble statue of Scotland's great historical novelist and poet. A winding stone staircase, very narrow in its upper reaches, leads to the top — 287 steps in all and well worth the climb.

From this fine viewpoint a marvellous panorama spreads out in all directions and down below are the tracks and platforms of Waverley. On 28 May 1966, a Black Five 4-6-0 pulls out with the 1045 to Birmingham, which would be combined with a train from Glasgow at Carstairs.

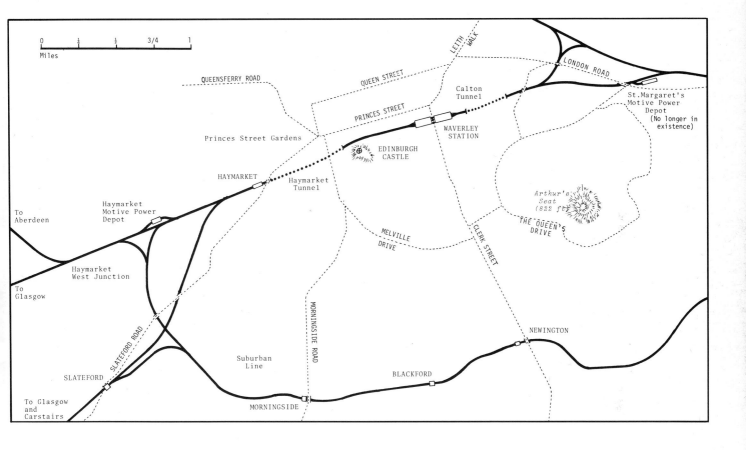

Edinburgh

96:
Nearing the end of its journey the Edinburgh portion of the 0900 Manchester to Glasgow and Edinburgh passes through West Princes Street Gardens on the approach to Waverley station on 27 May 1966. Double-heading was not uncommon on such trains simply as a means of running an engine with an unbalanced working back from Carstairs Jct. The locomotives in this instance are Black Five 4-6-0 44953 and an ex-LMS 2-6-4T.

This was a favourite boyhood observation point. Three footbridges spanned the shallow cutting and there were tunnels at either end. On summer Saturdays in the thirties there seemed to be a vast number of extra holiday trains and sometimes Haymarket depot would send down groups of locos coupled together to cut down on line occupation by light engine movements. As many as five or six, of quite varied types, were noted in a group. They would stop at this location and each would couple off and run through the short Mound Tunnel to its departure platform.

97:
East Princes Street Gardens provided equally good viewpoints right at the platform ends. Class B1 4-6-0 61148 comes round the south side of the station through Platform 21 with empty stock from Craigentinny carriage sidings, while BR Standard class 4 2-6-4T 80114 waits to leave Platform 11 on 6 June 1966.

61148 was in fact an old friend. Between 1950 and 1953 the author's place of work was close to Haymarket West Junction, where the connection to the Edinburgh suburban line leaves the main lines into Waverley. This route was taken by a great deal of freight traffic to Edinburgh from the north and west, and, of all the locomotives seen during this period, 61148 was noteworthy for the amazing regularity of its appearance on a mid-forenoon train. The working was observed most weekdays and seldom was it hauled by another engine. This B1 was shedded at Thornton at the time and had a return trip to Fife on an afternoon passenger. It was still at Thornton between 1962 and 1966 and it is conceivable that it was allocated to that depot for its whole working life.

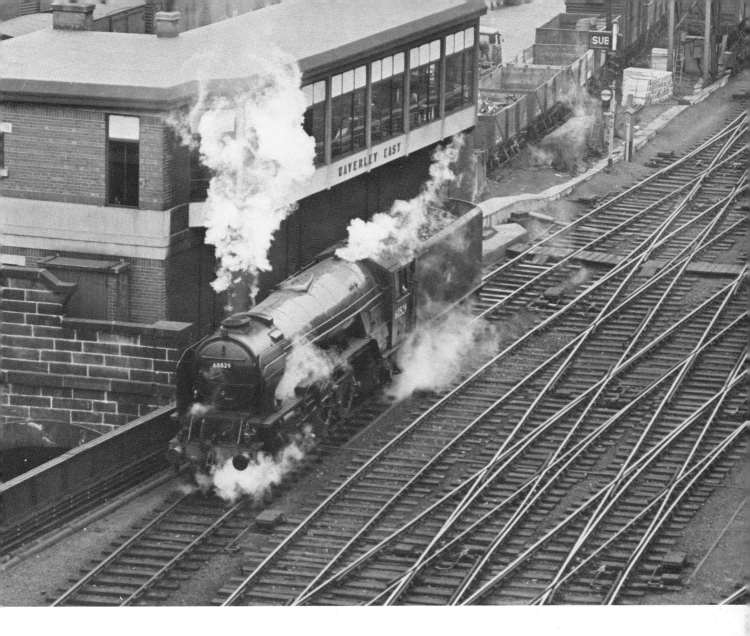

98-a:
An ex-LNER 0-6-0 of class J36 gets the road through the Suburban platform 21 at Edinburgh (Waverley) on 17 May 1961. The goods station dominates the background and the passenger station is off to the right. Introduced by Holmes of the NBR in 1888, this useful class eventually totalled 168. No less than 123 of them were taken into BR stock at the time of nationalization in 1948 and six of them survived until 1966 — the oldest having been in service for 75 years. The Government commandeered twenty-five of the J36s in 1917 for service in France and on return to Scotland they were given commemorative names. One of the war veterans, Maude (BR 65243) has been preserved by the Scottish Railway Preservation Society and is presently being restored at their Falkirk depot.

98-b:
Queen of Scots engine change at Waverley. This Pullman train ran between London (King's Cross) and Glasgow (Queen Street) via Leeds and Edinburgh, Pacifics of various classes being rostered for the duty. Class A4 60027 Merlin has just coupled off the arrival from Glasgow and is coming out of Platform 10 prior to running out to Haymarket loco. Sister engine 60011 Empire of India waits to take the train forward on the next leg to Newcastle at 1205 on 20 February 1961.

This viewpoint was reached through the Waverley Goods station. This was also where the Stationmaster parked his car and he usually went for lunch at noon. Walking down Platform 10, and customarily wearing his bowler hat, he would see that all was well with the Pullman before crossing the lines. A meeting with this austere gentleman was inevitable and on more than one occasion the author was asked if he was "a railway servant". A negative reply of course meant the gate. Polite requests to stay for just a few minutes until the Queen of Scots departed were countered with an equally polite, but extremely firm, suggestion that the picture could be taken from the platform. True, but then the two engines could not have been photographed side by side. Shed and lineside permits were willingly provided by BR in those days but stations and junctions were severely restricted.

99:
On 16 May 1961, it was a Peppercorn A2 which brought the Pullman from Glasgow. Here 60529 Pearl Diver, named, as so many LNER Pacifics were, after a racehorse, reverses away to Haymarket. The viewpoint for photograph 98-b is just to the right of the tender.

99

100:
St. Margarets loco depot was another favourite haunt
and the staff there were among the most friendly and
helpful people one could wish to meet. It was not
always so. During the war, the author was "ordered
off" (perhaps understandably) more times than he
cares to remember by one very officious individual,
but it was not too difficult to deduce which shift he
was on, and act accordingly.

The engines awaiting duty on 25 May 1965 are (l to
r) class A3 Pacific 60041 Salmon Trout, class B1
61029 Chamois, class A4 streamlined Pacific 60004
William Whitelaw, and BR Standard class 4 2-6-4T
80055. Looking on are George Cree (left), Locomotive Running Foreman and Willie Anderson, one
of his assistants.

101:
A visit to relatives in Parson's Green Terrace was
always relished as their flat overlooked the East Coast
main line and St. Margarets motive power depot. The
house was to the left of the row in the background in
this 1 July 1963 picture of ex-LNER class J38 65914.
By the time the author was photographically
equipped the relatives had unfortunately moved and
many potential "aerial" shots exist only in memory.
Perhaps someone more enterprising would have gone
to the house anyway and asked to use the front
room!

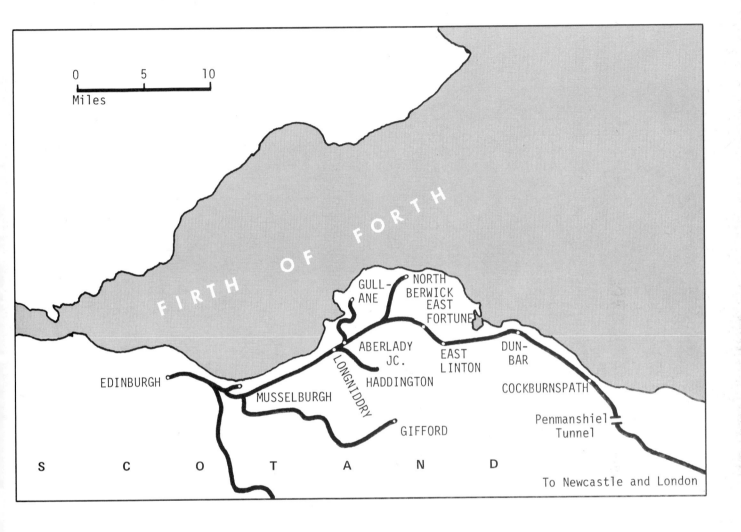

Miles

FIRTH OF FORTH

GULL-
ANE

NORTH
BERWICK
EAST
FORTUNE

ABERLADY
JC.

EAST
LINTON

DUN-
BAR

EDINBURGH

LONGNIDDRY

HADDINGTON

COCKBURNSPATH

MUSSELBURGH

GIFFORD

Penmanshiel
Tunnel

S   C   O   T   A   N   D

To Newcastle and London

102:
Wild spring flowers bloom prolifically along the
cutting beside Shandon Crescent, Edinburgh, as a BR
Standard class 4 2-6-4T climbs the curves between
Haymarket and Slateford with the 0820 Edinburgh-
Manchester. As with most Manchester, Liverpool and
Birmingham services it would be combined with a
portion from Glasgow at Carstairs Junction.

104:
An historic occasion on 1 May 1968. Ex-LNER class A3 Pacific 4472 Flying Scotsman, then 45 years old, arrives at Edinburgh (Waverley) after running non-stop from London (King's Cross) to commemorate the fortieth anniversary of the first non-stop run on the East Coast route between the two capital cities, a distance of 392.9 miles. This commemorative run was achieved only by virtue of the second tender, as many of the water troughs on the route had been removed by then. The locomotive on 1 May 1928 was also Flying Scotsman, hauling the train of the same name.

It was a miserably wet evening as 4472 emerged from the Calton Tunnel at the top of the 1 in 78 from St. Margarets but the exuberant use of the whistle as the train ran into Platform 10 made it obvious that the spirits of the crew, like those of the passengers and those of us who came to watch, could not be dampened by the worst of Scottish weather.

105:
The A3 Pacifics were a familiar sight on the East Coast main line for some forty years and it was quite appropriate that the last three of the class ended their lives working from St. Margarets shed, Edinburgh. The class underwent modification from time to time, one of which was the fitting of double chimneys. In this, the penultimate form, 60078 Night Hawk passes Longniddry, onetime junction with the Haddington branch, with a Sunday special express to Edinburgh from the south on 21 May 1961. The final version of the A3 was equipped with German Witte type smoke deflectors.

106:
It was a different story meteorologically on 4 May 1968 when Flying Scotsman made the return trip to London. Cockburnspath Bank, about forty miles from Edinburgh, had been chosen for photography and the weather could not have been more perfect — a warm, calm spring afternoon with primroses blooming discreetly along the cutting sides. The stacatto beat of the exhaust was heard to advantage here as the A3 climbed the 1 in 96 — over four miles of it and the steepest gradient on the East Coast route — and disappeared into Penmanshiel Tunnel near the top of the bank.

107:
In the early sixties Edinburgh's Haymarket loco depot kept many of its Pacifics particularly well groomed for working principal expresses. This is evident as class A4 60031 Golden Plover streaks through East Fortune with the 1100 Waverley to King's Cross in May 1961.

108-b:

An invitation from the signalman to join him in his cabin provided this vantage point from which to photograph class V2 2-6-2 60978 thundering through East Linton with freight for the Edinburgh area on 18 February 1961. Although not long after midday the winter sun casts very long shadows.

For many years, the V2s were one of the principal freight engines on the Scottish portion of the East Coast route, but being a true mixed traffic design they were also admirable performers on passenger trains.

108-a:

Another V2 hurries past East Fortune with a through freight for the south. This class was another of Gresley's 3-cylinder designs for the erstwhile LNER,

introduced in 1936 and still being built during the war. The design was no lightweight. Turning the scales at 93.1 tons (engine only) it was a mere 3 tons or so lighter than an A3 Pacific. In fact, the two classes had a great deal of similarity. Boiler pressures were 220 psi, but the V2 had 74" drivers while the A3's were 80". Cylinders were 18.5" x 26" and 19" x 26" respectively. The V2 however ended up with a slightly higher tractive effort at 33,730 lbs.

109:

A number of local services used to run east from Edinburgh for varying distances down the main line before turning off to serve several branch lines. There was one local service, however, which kept to the main line all the way – to Dunbar. On 18 February 1961, Ivatt class 2 2-6-0 46462, an ex-LMS immigrant to ex-LNER territory, slows for the stop at East Linton with the midday train.

Captions to photos appear on page 107.

110:
Amid the coastal farmlands of East Lothian, class J37 0-6-0 64586 plies to and fro with an engineer's train on Sunday 21 May 1961 near Aberlady Jct. This junction no longer exists because, like so many others, the branch line has been closed and lifted. The J37 was the North British Railway's largest 0-6-0 design and all 104 of the class, introduced in 1914, served the LNER throughout its 25 year existence and became British Rail stock. Although primarily freight engines, they were used not infrequently on passenger services.

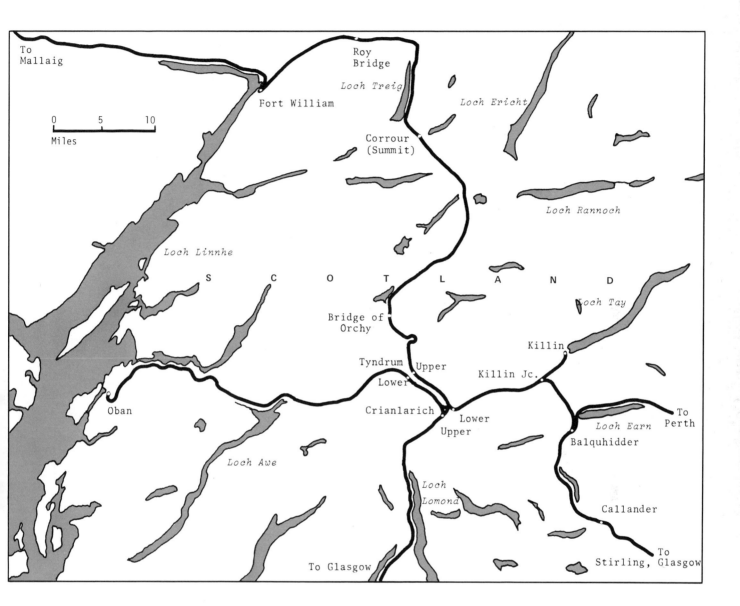

To
Mallaig

Roy
Bridge

Loch Treig

Fort William

Loch Ericht

0   5   10

Miles

Corrour
(Summit)

Loch Rannoch

Loch Linnhe

S   C   O   T   L   A   N   D

Loch Tay

Bridge of
Orchy

Tyndrum   Upper

Killin

Lower

Killin Jc.

Oban

Crianlarich   Lower
Upper

Loch Earn

To
Perth

Balquhidder

Loch Awe

*Loch
Lomond*

Callander

To Glasgow

To
Stirling, Glasgow

The Highlands

— where the scenery is just as alluring as the
steam and the weather just as variable

112:
For the Highlands, Crianlarich in Perthshire was a rather unique village in the railway sense. Like its neighbour Tyndrum, five miles to the west, it had two stations on different railways but it also had a junction layout linking the lines. True to Scottish custom the stations for both villages were named Upper and Lower strictly on the basis of altitude! Both "Uppers" were on the West Highland line which became, successively, the North British and LNER prior to nationalization. The "Lowers" were on the line of the former Callander and Oban Railway which subsequently became Caledonian Railway, LMS and then BR.

Making a spirited start out of Crianlarich (Upper) with the 1456 Fort William — Glasgow (Queen Street) in May 1961 are BR Standard class 5 4-6-0 73078 and Black Five 4-6-0 44956. The sound of this train was unforgettable. The evening was calm, the gradient 1 in 66 and the driving wheel diameters differed by 2″. The sharp bark of 73078 and the throatier exhaust of the Black Five blended and separated in a regular cycle as they made their way up to the head of Glen Falloch. In the ensuing stillness one wished the line was busier but it never did have more than two or three passenger trains each way daily at this location and freight service was far from intensive.

113:
Double heading was a common sight in the Scottish Highlands right up to the end of steam, not surprisingly with ruling gradients of 1 in 50 (2%). On the West Highland line of the former LNER from Glasgow (Queen St.) to Fort William, the pair in charge of a northbound passenger on 22 July 1960 are Black Five 44974 and class B1 61261 seen nearing the county march summit between Tyndrum and Bridge of Orchy. These two locomotive classes were perhaps the most comparable introduced by the two railway companies operating in Scotland prior to nationalization, the LMS and the LNER. Both could be considered their owners' "standard" 4-6-0 although the B1s were not introduced by the LNER until 1942, eight years after their rivals. The B1s were less numerous — only 410 against 842 LMS Black Fives. Boiler pressures were identical at 225 psi, driving wheel diameters varied by only 2″ and their weights differed by less than a ton. Both were in BR power class 5MT.

114:
Another West Highland scene — near Roy Bridge, in 1962. Although it is the month of May, snow lingers on the northern slopes of the mountains rising more than 3800 feet above sea level. Black Five 44787 gets under way with a Fort William — Glasgow freight and prepares to tackle sixteen miles of continuous climbing up Glen Spean and high above Loch Treig to the summit of the line at Corrour, 1350 ft. above sea level and the second highest standard gauge summit in Great Britain.

115:
Quietly oozing steam in the loop platform at Balquhidder, another Black Five 4-6-0 waits patiently with its freight for Oban until passenger trains in both directions have been given preference on the single line. This station, on the Callander and Oban route, was at one time a pleasant country junction with the line from the south approaching up 1 in 58. It then divided, with the main line continuing upwards at 1 in 60 while the branch dropped down through Lochearnhead and along the lochside to St. Fillans and Crieff. The very scenic stretch of the Oban line between Callander and Crianlarich has been closed and the Oban trains now run from Glasgow via the West Highland to Crianlarich Jct where they join the original route.

116:
A BR Standard class 4 2-6-4T 80092 leaves the Perthshire village of Killin with the 1352 to Killin Junction on the Oban line on 26 June 1963. Note the plump thrush on the left-hand rail cutting things a bit fine. It flew off in time!

The Killin branch, opened in 1886 and closed in 1965, was not much more than 5 miles long. After a short rise at 1 in 240 from the junction, which, incidentally, was away up on the hillside above Glen Dochart and not accessible by road, it dropped down at a uniform 1 in 50 to Killin (4 miles) and terminated at Loch Tay station. It was the last steam-operated branch in the Highlands, if not in all of Scotland.

In this sparsely populated area, one of the branch engine's duties was to get the high school pupils down to Callander in the morning and bring them back in the afternoon, which gave it four journeys of 19 miles on the main line, two of which were light engine.

117:
The ubiquitous Black Fives again! 44959 is paired up with 45400 on the 1205 Oban – Glasgow (Buchanan Street) seen restarting after taking water on 3 May 1961. The line from Callander to Oban ran in a rough L shape, northwards at first and then west. Among the hills of Perthshire and Argyll it was anything but straight, which resulted in the westbound line through Balquhidder actually heading north-east. The unfamiliar traveller could be further confused by the fact the Balquhidder East signal cabin was at the south-west end of the station! It would seem that when the line was built, between 1866 and 1880, everything in the Oban direction was considered westward despite what the compass said.

118:
According to the Handbook for Railway Steam Locomotive Enginemen published by the British Transport Commission in 1957, this A4 Pacific is being perfectly fired judging by the light-grey smoke. Perth General station is seen in the background as 60034 Lord Faringdon storms through the complex layout and is about to pass the locomotive depot on its right with the 1330 Aberdeen – Glasgow (Buchanan Street) on 2 June 1966.

After nationalization of the railways in 1948, there was a distinct tendency for LMS practices to be adopted and for locomotives of that company to infiltrate areas that were formerly owned by rival companies at the expense of the latter companies' engines. In opposition to this trend, the principal ex-LMS passenger services between Glasgow and Aberdeen were taken over almost exclusively by ex-LNER Pacifics in the final years of steam in Scotland. Other services on the route such as the legendary West Coast Postal and the fast fish trains from Aberdeen were similarly powered during this period.

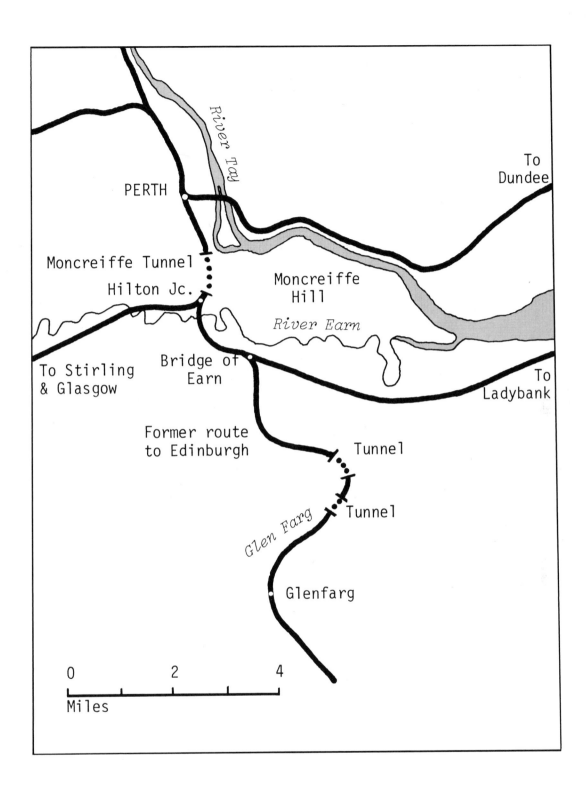

Perth

— where a considerable variety of fine
viewpoints is available in a small area.

121:
Britannia Pacific 70005 John Milton bursts into daylight at the south portal of the Moncreiffe tunnel on 19 May 1965. Despite its proximity to public roads this location was not at all obvious and means of access had to be diligently sought out. From a quiet little road which ran over the tunnel an obscure footpath led to a ladder down the masonry retaining wall, just visible at the left of the picture on the opposite page. One could also gain access from the main Perth-Edinburgh road by taking the road to a farm from which an unpaved lane led to the junction. After several visits without incident there was one occasion when the author and a friend found their way out blocked by a farm tractor. A polite request at the farmhouse to have the tractor moved was greeted with a bit of a tirade to the effect that the farmer was "fed up wi' you trainspotters". Apparently, enough people had discovered this access that vehicular traffic was becoming a nuisance! A bit of quick thinking suggested that this was the only way that railway maintenance crews could reach the junction by road so it was pointed out that "some work had to be done up at the box". At once his whole attitude changed and the tractor was quickly whisked out of the way. Possibly BR was paying him something for right of entry! Incidentally the road was not marked "Private".

120:
A short distance south of Perth lies Hilton Junction. It isn't an unusual layout — simply the divergence of two double track main lines — but the topography makes it interesting. It is just south of a ridge separating the valleys of the Earn and the Tay, on which river Perth is situated, and the railway penetrates this ridge by means of the Moncreiffe Tunnel.

On 1 June 1966, one of Aberdeen's stud of A4 Pacifics, 60019 Bittern, is about to disappear beneath the photographer's feet as it approaches off the line from Glasgow and Stirling with the 0825 Buchanan Street — Aberdeen. The line is clear for a train in the opposite direction bound for Edinburgh. While the junction still exists today, Edinburgh services now take the long way round via the Glasgow line as far as Larbert, as the former LNER route through Glenfarg has been closed.

122:
The Hilton Junction signal box is visible at the extreme left as A4 60019 Bittern accelerates the 1330 from Aberdeen round the curve in the Glasgow direction. The steam nicely separates the locomotive from the lower slopes of Moncreiffe Hill behind. The Edinburgh line can be seen beyond the engine at the right.

123:
On the left, the 1408 Aberdeen-London (Broad Street) fish heads south out of Perth behind 70038 Robin Hood, one of the BR Standard Britannia class Pacifics of which 55 were built, starting in 1951. Approaching the camera is a Black Five on its way from the sheds to Perth Yard to pick up a freight working. The road bridge in the distance provided the viewpoint for the photograph on page 118.

Captions to photos next page:

124-a:
Moncreiffe Hill again provides the background on 19 May 1965 with Class B1 4-6-0 61330 taking the Edinburgh line at Hilton Junction. Soon the engine will be faced with the stiff climb to Glenfarg — 6 miles of 1 in 75.

124-b:
The B1s had a purposeful air about them, as was amply demonstrated by 61133 working hard up Glenfarg bank on a warm calm evening in May 1966. The train is the 1830 Perth-Thornton freight consisting mainly of coal empties.

Although designed for mixed traffic duties, it was quite a sprightly looking engine and, indeed, the first forty of the class were named after various types of antelope. The B1s were originally referred to as the Antelopes but this term fell into disuse as the bulk of the later engines were unnamed.

Note the different types of track. The line on the right still has bull-headed rail, chairs and keys, while that on the left has been relaid with flat-bottomed rail held in place by more modern fastenings.

Captions to 124-a and 124-b appear on page 123.
Caption to 125-b appears on page 126.

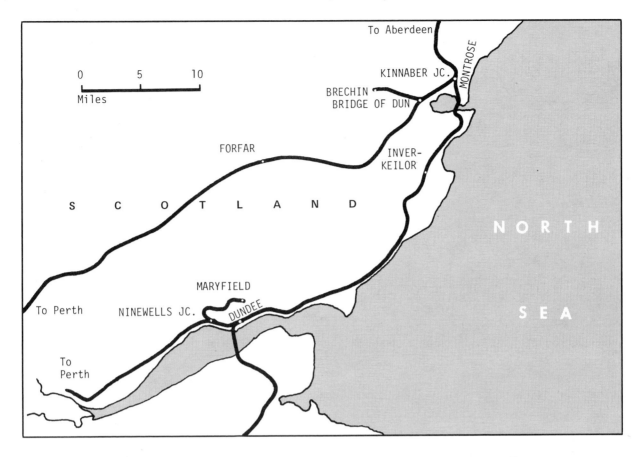

Dundee and Northwards

125 and 126:
One of the last strongholds of the J37 0-6-0s was Dundee where the survivors continued to work on local freight until 1966. Situated on the shore of the Firth of Tay just outside Dundee, the delightfully-named Ninewells Junction provides the setting as 64602 leaves the main line with coal for Maryfield (page 125) and returns with empties (above).

This W.P. Reid (NBR) design was simple and robust. In all, 104 were built between 1914 and 1921, 35 by the company's own workshops at Cowlairs and the remainder by the North British Locomotive Company Ltd. at their Atlas Works in Glasgow. Although slight variations existed at building, boiler pressure was eventually standardized at 180 psi. This coupled with two 19½" x 26" cylinders and 60" drivers gave a tractive effort of 25,210 lbs, a very respectable figure for an engine weighing a little under 55 tons. Coal and water capacities were 7 tons and 3500 gals respectively giving a tender weight in working order of 41 tons. 64602 was one of the 1919 batch from North British Locomotive Company.

127:
As late as 1965, a Dundee J37 was still entrusted with a daily main line turn to Montrose and back. On 27 May of that year, 64597, another of the 1919 engines, steams across the rolling farmland near Inverkeilor as a herd of cattle go up the road in the background for milking.

128:
60007 Sir Nigel Gresley sweeps across the switched diamonds of Kinnaber Jct. with the 0710 Aberdeen to Glasgow (Buchanan Street) on 20 May 1965.

At this historic spot the East Coast and West Coast routes from London to Aberdeen converged and it was a crucial point in the Railway Race to the North in 1895. Whoever was first at Kinnaber was first at Aberdeen.

Sir Nigel is taking the West Coast route (Caledonian) through Forfar, Perth and Stirling as far as Glenboig where it will diverge to Glasgow. Nearer the camera the North British part of the East Coast route leaves the Caledonian main line to reach Montrose, Dundee and Edinburgh. It is interesting to note that even in the sixties the signalmen at Kinnaber still referred to the lines as the "Caley" and the NB, despite the fact that these companies were absorbed in the Grouping of 1923 into the then new LMS and LNER respectively.

Things are greatly changed today. The "Caley" has been closed for some years and trains reach Perth via the NB line and Dundee. A single line was left in for four miles as far as Bridge of Dun to allow the Brechin branch to continue in use for freight traffic.

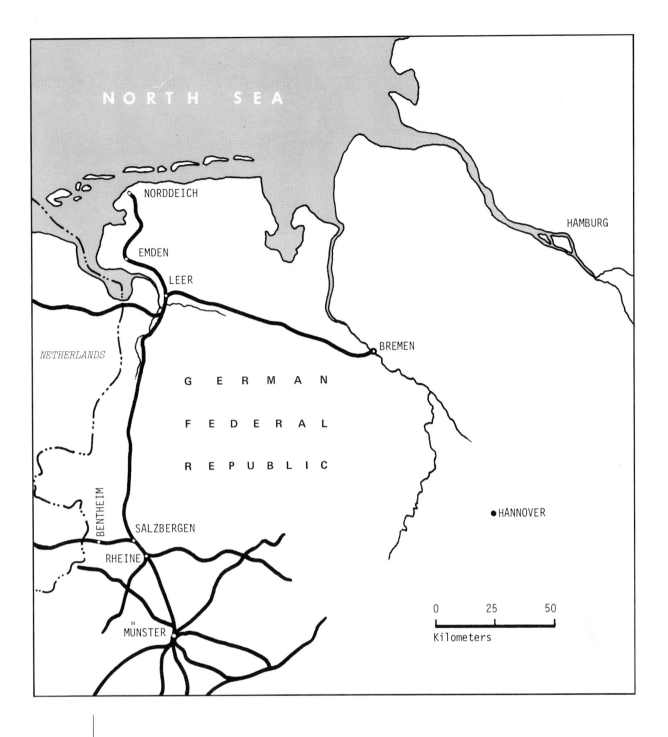

5 | WEST GERMANY

West Germany in 1972 had much to offer the steam enthusiast. Membership in railway societies, all but one of which owns one or more locomotives and one of which has an operating line, suggests that the author is not against preservation! However, after a few years of preserved steam only in Canada and Great Britain, it was refreshing to see once again steam locomotives earning their coal and water as part of a fully commercial enterprise — and not relegated to secondary services either. They were spread over the whole country and working hand-in-hand with other forms of motive power, and in some instances "under the wires". The Deutsche Bundesbahn at that time had some 1400 "Dampfloks", of which close to 1200 were 2-10-0s.

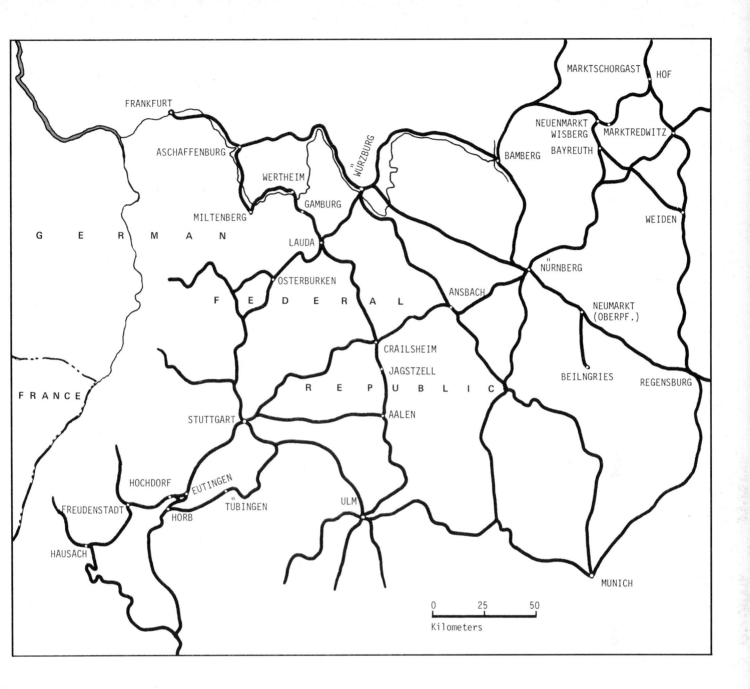

130:
The North Sea ports, as could be expected, generate vast quantities of rail traffic. One of these is Emden, in the extreme northwest of the country. A little farther north lies Norddeich whence large modern ferries operate a frequent service to the East Friesian Islands. This combination results in an intensive passenger and freight service southwards through Rheine and Münster to numerous destinations.

On 18 September 1972, all was apparently not well at Rheine as many trains were being stopped at the pleasant little crossing at Bentlage, the next "Blockstelle" up the line. The location, selected for photographing trains accelerating away from Rheine, was therefore fortuitously chosen, as southbound trains, which would normally have been running easily or coasting were heard to much better advantage.

Here a class 012 Pacific restarts one of the Norddeich boat trains after being checked. The sound of this fine 3-cylinder oil-fired Pacific was an absolute delight.

Germany

132:
On 19 September 1972, class 012 Pacific 012 068-3 storms away from a stop at Salzbergen with the 1222 Leer to Münster local.

Typical DB signals can be seen on the right, while the station and junction are visible at the upper left. The line swinging off to the right beyond the station is that to Emden and Norddeich; the straight ahead route leads to Bentheim and the Netherlands.

133-a:
In September 1972, the turntable at Rheine "Bahnbetriebswerk" was under repair which accounted for some tender first running in the area. Easily distinguishable from a distance by its positively enormous chimney, oil-fired class 042 2-8-2 042 164-4 approaches Salzbergen with a northbound freight. This was the only DB class of Mikado at the time. Note the superb track and deep ballast, so typical throughout West Germany.

133-b:
If ever there was a locomotive cemetery, the headstones for DB engines could be provided by simply taking one cabside panel of each and mounting it on a suitable post or stand — there is so much information there! Information is provided relating to brakes and valve gear for this coal-fired 2-10-0 in addition to its region (Bahndirektion Münster) and depot allocation (Bahnbetriebswerk Emden).

134-a:
Rounding a curve in the road along the south side of the winding Main valley on 26 September 1972, a pall of smoke was seen across the valley beyond the shoulder of a hill. The railway at this point was on the far side of the river. The source of the smoke proved indeed to be emanating from a "Dampflok" which was coupled up to a train of hoppers at what appeared to be a gravel pit or quarry. Departure seemed imminent and not many minutes elapsed before the 2-10-0 moved off, with its white plume mirrored in the rippled waters of the River Main.

134-b.:
One of the compact 2-6-2Ts of class 064 waits to leave Miltenberg with the 1735 for Aschaffenburg on 25 September 1972. Miltenberg, a pleasant little town on the River Main, is graced with two stations and an interesting double junction. The Hauptbahnhof (main station) is a terminus but through trains call there on the secondary route to and from Lauda in addition to passing through the Nord station. Reversal is therefore necessary for the short distance to and from the junction. A cross country route branches off southwards to Osterburken. The frequent local service between the larger centre of Aschaffenburg and Miltenberg was being worked turn and turn about by the class 064 2-6-2Ts and 2-10-0s of classes 050, 051 or 052.

135:
Vineyards can be seen on the hillside above the locomotive as a class 051 2-10-0 takes the 1549 to Aschaffenburg out of Miltenberg on 25 September 1972. The passenger stock on many local services consists, as here, of six-wheel coaches of quite modern appearance.

137: *(opposite)*
The mediaeval town of Wertheim stands at the confluence of the River Tauber and the River Main. A heavy freight, after a stop at Wertheim yards, is taking the Tauber valley line to Lauda behind one of the prolific DB 2-10-0s. A fortunate little plume of steam from the safety valves sets off the top of the boiler and the chimney from the background. The line diverging on the right goes to Lohr where it joins the electrified Aschaffenburg – Würzburg line.

The locomotive is a two-cylinder design introduced in 1938 of which several hundreds were still at work on the DB in 1972 on freight and local passenger work. Classes 050, 051 and 052 were generally similar and were limited to a maximum speed of 80 kmph.

136: *(opposite)*

Local passenger services from Lauda were in the hands of both tank and tender locomotives, of classes 064 and 023 respectively, on 26 September 1972. The 1501 Lauda-Wertheim, seen approaching Gamburg, requires 2-6-2 023 059-9 to run tender first northbound due to the absence of turning facilities at Wertheim.

The practice of hooking a van of perishables or other urgent merchandise on the tail end of a passenger train, a common sight in Britain for so many years, is seen here in its modern form — an ISO container on a flat car.

139:
In 1972, a pocket of Pacific working centred around Hof, near the East German frontier. The locomotives concerned were all of class 001 and with a permissible speed of 130 kmph they were diagrammed for all fast passenger workings on the line to Bamberg, home of the celebrated symphony orchestra, as well as services on the Regensburg line.

About half-way between Bamberg and Hof is the junction at Neuenmarkt-Wirsberg where eastbound trains are faced with a rather formidable climb known as the Schiefe Ebene — 10km at 1 in 40 — up to Marktschorgast. It is not surprising that rear-end assistance was provided on most trains, with the banker dropping off in Marktschorgast station. Driver's discretion and existence of a stop at Neuenmarkt-Wirsberg apparently had some influence on whether assistance was taken or not.

Amid the woodlands of Northern Bavaria, 001 202-1 tackles the Schiefe Ebene unaided with the 1320 Bamberg-Hof on 28 September 1972. This particular engine was built by Henschel in 1937, although the class was introduced in 1926.

138:
Markschorgast station in Northern Bavaria is the location as the 1552 Hof-Bamberg approaches quietly out of the murk behind class 001 Pacific 001 168-4 and is about to descend the Schiefe Ebene. A striking feature of DB steam locomotives is their quietness when drifting and one must keep a sharp look-out while on the lineside, especially in thick fog as on 27 September 1972. Unlike the class 012 Pacifics operating in the northern part of the country, the 001s are 2-cylinder machines (23.6" x 26"). Driving wheel diameter is 78.75" and boiler pressure 227 psi.

140:
The line singles at Marktschorgast and still climbing, but not so steeply, winds its way round a curve which gives the impression that it is almost a horse-shoe but is really a deep vee with a round base.

Because of the stiff eastbound gradients most freight avoids this line as an alternative more easily graded route is available via Marktredwitz. However as the fog lifts on 28 September 1972, a class 052 2-10-0 blasts its way uphill with a freight for Hof. The line was completely invisible from this viewpoint on the previous day!

141:
Weiden (Oberpf) is a major railway centre on the line between Regensburg and Hof. Perusal of the timetables revealed the simultaneous departure of two northbound passenger trains at 1320, one for Hof scheduled for Pacific haulage and another taking the secondary route northeastward via Kirchenlaibach to Bayreuth. The latter turned out to be a 2-6-2T duty, class 064.

Precision is a key word in West Germany and nowhere more apparent than on the DB, where meticulous attention is paid to timekeeping. The station clocks have second hands! With this in mind, it was a virtual certainty that the two 1320 trains would leave exactly together on the multi-track layout. They did. The guards' whistles were only seconds apart and not unexpectedly, the crews indulged in a little competition as far as the the divergence of the two routes. Pacific 001 181-7 (left) was actually on the move first, but only just, and 064 295-9 with its lighter train was accelerating marginally more quickly until, on passing this viewpoint, it slipped violently and lost a little of its apparent advantage. The eventual "winner" is not known but the two engines and their crews made a fine spirited start. The date — 29 September 1972.

142:
Under the catenary at the Nürnberg suburban station at Dutzendteich is a 3-cylinder 2-10-0 of class 044 bound for Nürnberg Rangiersbahnhof (freight yard). A pre-breakfast sortie on 2 October 1972 had produced a number of interesting pictures in the low morning sunlight although all steam hauled traffic (strictly freight in this area) had been northbound and consequently strongly backlit. The call of the stomach had prevailed and the cameras had been stowed, when the unmistakable chant of three cylinders was heard close at hand — one of those quiet approach situations with steam shut off. Apparently the train had been running under "caution" signals and the driver had opened up as he got a clear road at the north end of the station. There was just time to get the camera from its case and precious little else!

The 044s of which some 2000 existed in 1945, have 21.6" x 26" cylinders, and 55" coupled wheels.

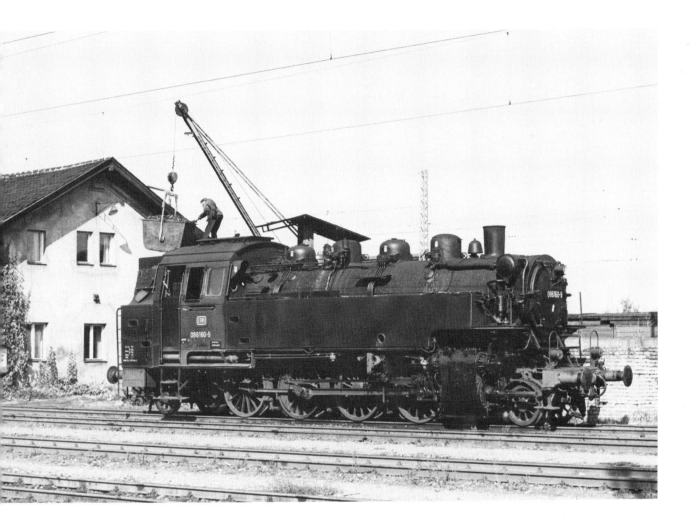

143:
Some 40 km south-east of Nürnberg in a very pleasant part of Bavaria, a branch leaves the Regensburg line at Neumarkt (Oberpf) and runs south for about 28 km to Beilngries. 086 160-9, one of a pair of Nürnberg Bw 2-8-2T engines of class 086 subshedded at the junction for working the branch, has its bunker replenished at the Neumarkt coaling stage after arrival with the 1205 from Beilngries.

Several ungated level crossings on this branch enable the locomotive whistle to be heard — an infrequent sound on the DB. Departures are not heralded by a "highball" as in North America or even a discreet "pip" as in the UK; neither are friendly whistles dispensed to lineside enthusiasts; it is strictly a warning device.

In rural areas such as this, a high proportion of railway travellers were found to be school children. With the precise train operation mentioned earlier, dawdling was frowned on and the students were expected to board the train smartly, as witness one guard walking down the platform shouting "Blitz! Blitz!" — at 0630 one crisp autumn morning!

144:
The terminus at Beilngries has a lovely station building, quite imposing for the size of town it serves. On a mellow October afternoon in 1972, 2-8-2T 086 534-5 has just coupled off the 1335 from Neumarkt, composed of two bogie coaches and two six-wheelers, and goes to run round.

145:
Class 023 2-6-2 023 031-8 at speed near Jagstzell with the 1721 Crailsheim – Aalen on 4 October 1972. The valley of the River Jagst at this point is not a deep one but the autumn sun had dipped low enough to cast shadows of the western hills across the whole valley and sunlit photographs were over for that day. This dictated the choice of a high angle viewpoint to set off the steam against a darker background and the opportunity was taken to pan as the location and anticipated train speed seemed to be very suitable.

Like the class 086 2-8-2Ts, the 023 2-6-2s were introduced in 1950 and only the class 065 large 2-6-4Ts of the DB steam locomotives were of more recent origin, and by only one year.

147: *(opposite)*
The oldest design in existence on the DB in 1972 was the class 038 4-6-0, introduced by the Prussian State Railways in 1906 as class P8. The last seven of the class were allocated to the depot at Tübingen for local passenger services. There were early morning and evening workings along the main line between Horb and Böblingen, a short distance south-west of Stuttgart.

On 6 October 1972, 038 772-0 worked the 1110 Eutingen-Freudenstadt and is seen near Hochdorf. The engine gave the appearance of being very well cared for and every steam joint was as tight as a drum.

146: *(opposite)*
This photograph was completely unplanned — a case of shooting and hoping. A featherweight load for one of the **DB** 2 cylinder 2-10-0s but a most pleasant sight in the mellow morning sunlight.

At Horb the double track Stuttgart-Konstanz route is joined by the single line from Tübingen, the tracks running on opposite sides of the Neckar valley as they approach the town from the east. It was while driving up a narrow road in search of viewpoints along this valley that steam suddenly burst into view. There was just enough time to stop the car, guess the exposure and shoot. Just as well — it was the only steam at Horb all forenoon!

Perhaps the abundance of DB 2-10-0s could make one complacent, but with hundreds of the 2-cylinder variety around it presents a greater challenge to capture one which for reasons of angle, location, lighting and steam effect, is unlike any other. There seems little doubt that the last DB steam locomotives in regular service will be 2-10-0s.

148:
The delightful town of Freudenstadt in the Black Forest has a spacious station layout and a large locomotive depot, testimony to days of heavier traffic. On 6 October 1972, the local passenger to Hausach was still steam-hauled, by the same engine which had brought the forenoon train over from Eutingen.

At the sharply curved south end of the station, 038 772-0, with cylinder cocks wide open, reverses coaches into the station to form the 1404 to Hausach.

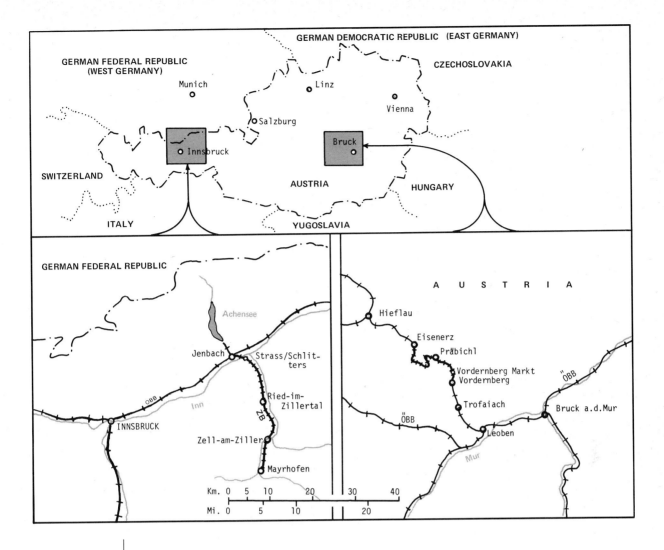

6

AUSTRIA:

A POSTSCRIPT

Austria, a romantic and smiling land populated by a warm, unaffected, fun-loving (and well-fed!) people, is a "must" on the European itinerary of anyone seeking the quaint and the unusual in steam railway operations. Main line operations are concentrated in the eastern area of the country near Vienna, but there are a number of isolated operations elsewhere, such as the standard-gauge rack railway serving the Erzberg, the *iron mountain* at Eisenerz, and the 30"-gauge Zillertalbahn in the Tyrol a short distance from Innsbruck, which are portrayed here.

Though both are located in the high Alps, they stand in strong contrast to one another from a topographical standpoint. The Eisenerz operation, a part of the far-flung ÖBB or Austrian Federal Railways network, utilizes grades up to 8% to raise the railway over a 1200-metre Alpine summit in 21 km. between Vordernberg and Eisenerz. Its tranquil counterpart is the quaint Zillertalbahn which extends 32 km. between Jenbach and Mayrhofen in the flat, fertile and pretty valley of the Ziller. The ZB is a splendid example of a local light railway built for economic reasons rather than through the dictates of topography. Its opposite termini are less than 100 m. different in altitude.

As noted in the preface, the accompanying photographs were edited and printed by the late Charles Bowman following his Austrian visit in September 1974.

A

B

C

150-a:

An *alp* or mountain meadow interrupts the forested hillside above Zillertalbahn locomotive No. 3, *Tirol*, as it hurries along the Ziller valley near Strass/Schlitters with the 1045 Jenbach-Mayrhofen train on 28 September 1974. The cars are divided into first- and second-class accommodation. Note the triangular plaque on the second car from the locomotive which signifies that it is a *Nichtraucher* — non-smoking — car. The train hustles along at a respectable speed, taking one hour and eight minutes to perform its 20-mile journey, including fourteen intermediate stops. The ZB was constructed between 1900 and 1902.

150-b, 150-c, 151:

A standard-gauge covered van on a transporter wagon forms the backdrop for No. 3 *Tirol* of the Zillertalbahn, a narrow-gauge 0-6-2T stopped at Zell-am-Ziller on 27 September 1974 with the 1550 passenger train from Jenbach to Mayrhofen. As the oversized cylinder suggests, No. 3 is a compound, a rare breed even in Europe. This bustling and spotless miniature locomotive, built by Krauss at Linz, Austria in 1902, was in its 73rd year when the photograph was made, proudly carrying the marks of its "family" and ancestry on spotless brass plates backgrounded in crimson enamel.

152:
ZB No. 3, *Tirol*, arriving at Zell-am-Ziller with the nine-car 1550 Jenbach-Mayrhofen on 27 September 1974. The high- and low-pressure cylinders can be recognized by the small and large cylinder covers.

153:
The Zillertalbahn caters to its large tourist-season following by operating a "drive-yourself" train for amateur engineers. This train, comprising a small, industrial-sized locomotive and two cars which are playhouse-sized even in contrast to the ZB's small rolling stock, can be chartered for various periods of time. The operation, which is fitted in as extra movements between regularly-scheduled trains, operates from the inland terminus at Mayrhofen to Zell-am-Ziller, shown here, a distance of 8 km. Needless to say, a fully-qualified locomotive engine-man accompanies the guest-driver on the footplate, to ensure that regular trains are neither impeded nor delayed.

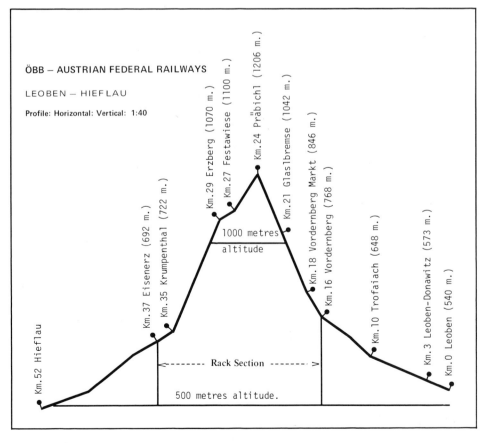

ÖBB – AUSTRIAN FEDERAL RAILWAYS

LEOBEN – HIEFLAU

Profile: Horizontal: Vertical: 1:40

Km.52 Hieflau

Km.37 Eisenerz (692 m.)
Km.35 Krumpenthal (722 m.)
Km.29 Erzberg (1070 m.)
Km.27 Festawiese (1100 m.)
Km.24 Präbichl (1206 m.)
Km.21 Glaslbremse (1042 m.)
Km.18 Vordernberg Markt (846 m.)
Km.16 Vordernberg (768 m.)
Km.10 Trofaiach (648 m.)
Km.3 Leoben-Donawitz (573 m.)
Km.0 Leoben (540 m.)

1000 metres altitude

Rack Section

500 metres altitude.

154:
Austrian Federal Railways (ÖBB) 0-6-2T No. 97.209, assisted by sister No. 97.208 at the rear, lifts a rake of four-wheeled ore empties up the 8% grade of the *Erzbergbahn* north of Vordernberg Markt on 26 September 1974. This line once operated twelve-coupled locomotives which are reputed to have been the largest steam rack locomotives ever constructed.

155:
A crag of the Erzberg, the iron ore mountain, dominates the background as No. 97.217 pushes the 1239 Vordernberg-Hieflau passenger train north of Vordernberg Markt on 26 September 1974. The locomotive remains on the downgrade end of the passenger train movements. At the top of the grade at Präbichl, the locomotive will run around the train to the head end for the descent into Eisenerz. Note that the car ahead of the locomotive is a *nichtraucher*. The Giesl ejector smokestack is a prominent feature of the Eisenerz locomotives.

157: *(opposite)*

Shortly after the photograph on page 155 was taken, the 1239 Vordernberg-Hieflau leaves Präbichl with No. 97.217 in its conventional position at the head of the train. The passenger train having cleared the single-track main line, a loaded ore train, with 97.209 on the nearer, rear end, and 97.208 heading the train at the opposite end, prepare to begin the descent to Vordernberg. A train of empties, headed by a diesel-hydraulic rack locomotive then on trial and trailed by an 0-6-2T, is about to clear the loaded ore train, following the passenger train down into Eisenerz.

156: *(opposite)*

A view at Präbichl, at the top of the pass, as No. 97.209, assisted by No. 97.208 at the rear, moves a train of ore empties into the clear. No. 97.207, at right at the head of a loaded train, waits to descend to Vordernberg. The ore is destined for the Donawitz steel works at Leoben, 14 km. beyond Vordernberg.

POSTLUDE

STEAM, BY ITS VERY NATURE, cannot visibly last long when released to the atmosphere unless of course there is a constant source of supply. It would appear that a sufficient number of people in many parts of the world are prepared to make sacrifices of hours, effort and money to enable steam to be produced in locomotive boilers for many a foreseeable year. Neither can these people last forever but their endeavours must inevitably inspire future generations so that the human race will never see the end of the "white plume".

158:
No. 4472 *Flying Scotsman* pulling *Bulmer's Cider Express* at the site of Chinley East Junction on 25 September 1973, bound from Manchester to Sheffield.

160:
DB No. 023-067-2 leaving Heilbronn Hauptbahnhof with the 1207 to Schwäbische Hall, on 8 October 1972.